Man... ...government

KING ALFRED'S ...
WIN...

Organisational Behaviour in Local Government

Dr Ita O'Donovan

General Editors:
Michael Clarke and John Stewart

WITHDRAWN FROM
THE LIBRARY

UNIVERSITY OF
WINCHESTER

KA 0246407 1

KING ALFRED'S COLLEGE
WINCHESTER

02460071 | 352.042
OLD

Published by Longman Information and Reference,
Longman Group Limited, 6th Floor,
Westgate House, The High, Harlow, Essex CM20 1YR
Telephone: Harlow (0279) 442601; Fax: Harlow (0279) 444501;
Telex: 81491 Padlog.

© Longman Group Limited 1994
All righs reserved. No part of this publication may be reproduced, stored in a retrieval system, or transmitted in any form or by any means, electronic mechanical, photocopying, recording or otherwise, without the prior permission of the Copyright owner or a licence permitting restricted copying issued by the Copyright Licensing Agency Ltd., 90 Tottenham Court Road, London W1P 9HE.

A catalogue record for this book is available from the British Libarary
ISBN 0-582-25134-6

Printed and bound in Great Britain by Bookcraft (Bath) Ltd.

Contents

■ ACKNOWLEDGEMENTS

I should like to thank several people for their assistance in completing this book: Donald Curtis for his insightful comments and suggestions as the book began to take shape; my colleagues Steve Freer, Andrew Lawrence, David Mason, James Parry and Katrina Ritters at Warwickshire County Council who influenced my thinking about organisational behaviour in local government; Julie Sturgess who most generously helped me to come to some understanding of layout principles; the series editors, Michael Clarke and John Stewart, who read and commented on the draft of this book; and, finally, my family, Frank, Eoin and Yvonne, who always had time for this book to intrude into their lives.

Introduction

■ MY PURPOSE

The purpose of this book is to examine the organisational behavioural aspects of the changes in the local government environment, with the aim of increasing local government officers' personal and organisational effectiveness. Local government has experienced a massive amount of change in the last fifteen years. The collective policy and operational consequences of the changes in local government as a whole have been well documented and analysed. Irrespective of how we evaluate the changes in terms of policy, it is clear that they have had an enormous effect on the organisational strategies, structures and systems of individual local governments. In simple terms the environment in which local government officers work and the content and process of the individual jobs that they perform have undergone considerable changes.

Success in local government is closely aligned to two strengths, expert knowledge of a subject area and management of human resources. In the past, and some would argue still today, promotional success in local government has been heavily weighted towards rewarding professional competence, assuming that it was accompanied by managerial competence. This book concentrates on the latter in recognition of the fact that it is people who achieve an organisation's goals, purposes and outputs.

I am advocating the need for managers to be more 'literate' about their work environment, to understand, to anticipate better the likely behavioural outcomes of the interaction between people and organisational settings. Simply put, this means knowing how and why things get done and who gets them done. This book is about gaining extra sensitivity to work processes so that the individual and organisational performance may be more effective. The book is therefore addressed to the local government manager. It invites her/him to explore the content and process elements of organisational behaviour in local government.

■ READER'S GUIDE

Since the main purpose of the book is to increase the reader's personal and organisational effectiveness, the choice of chapters was influenced by the author's experience as practitioner and consultant in local government and her familiarity with the range of issues in which senior managers become involved. Thus the book moves from an exploration of the local government environment represented by its cultures, to the individual as a manager in the workplace, to the numerous strategic and operational issues that local government managers face in the course of their working life.

Chapter 1 makes the point that managers in local government must take account of the way organisational culture/s have been used to shape the local government working environment. The changes in local government are analysed in cultural terms. Understanding organisational culture is seen as essential to being an effective manager.

Chapter 2 introduces the manager to a framework for analysing individual organisational behaviour. It focuses on two dimensions. The manager's ability to understand large 'P' and small 'p' political environments and the degree to which the manager takes account of self and others. Understanding yourself as a manager is seen as an essential ingredient to managing others.

Chapter 3 emphasises the need for managers to achieve effective work outcomes from groups. The dynamics of group behaviour are explored together with the roles people play in groups. The factors a manager must consider when managing and structuring groups are discussed.

Chapter 4 looks at the issue of recruitment and selection from the perspective of a manager seeking to appoint the most effective performer to the post. The chapter examines how a manager ensures the fulfilment of the critical requirements needed for a vacant post. A variety of selection tools that may help in the selection decision are discussed. The difficulties inherent in the interview process are analysed from the perspective of the manager.

Chapter 5 examines how people are motivated to perform at work. It looks at content and process theories of motivation and how they have been applied in the new management of local government.

Chapter 6 outlines the broad framework of performance management in local government and the range of skills it requires from managers. The chapter then looks more closely at individual methods of appraisal and the skills required by managers to appraise staff.

Chapter 7 sets individual management development within the context of a strategy for corporate management development in an authority. The importance of managers' participation in defining and designing the management development requirements of staff is stressed, as well as the managers' support for staff engaged in management development activities. The relevance of learning to authorities and managers is discussed at length.

Chapter 8 explores the management of change and the role of the manager in facilitating a successful change process. It strongly makes the point that change is not in any sense a linear process but rather a dynamic interactive process which requires a participatory approach from managers.

1

Organisational culture

Key points

◆ *Culture is a key factor in any organisational change process.*

◆ *To understand a culture you must explore its core elements.*

◆ *Local governments have used the concept of corporate culture as an agent for change.*

◆ *Managers involved in bringing about change must understand the culture of their operating environment.*

■ INTRODUCTION

This chapter pursues the idea that understanding the concept of culture and, more narrowly, the different cultures within local government is essential for managers who wish to understand organisational behaviour. Many local governments have explored the culture of their organisations. Some have sought to bring about change by clarifying or changing some of the core elements of their culture. Organisations and local authorities have been interested in the concept of corporate culture because they realise that organisational culture can socialise the behaviour of employees. Culture has been seen as a way of integrating employees into the organisation and encouraging behaviour in tune with the objectives of the organisation.

What is interesting to you as managers in local government is how culture, which is a human product, is being used by different local authorities to change the atmosphere within which employees operate. Culture in this way is being used as a change agent because it has been largely assumed that corporate culture can improve organisational effectiveness. Local authorities are developing and have developed unique individual cultures in an attempt to socialise employees into fostering the beliefs, values and norms of the organisation. Such an approach is seen as a way towards increased performance as officers become aware of the 'Common Goal' and become more economic, efficient and effective at each level. Before we explore the kinds of changes that have been taking place it would be useful to look briefly at the concept of culture and at some of the core elements of culture, within the context of what we now term traditional local government. We cannot understand or evaluate the changes unless we look first at the history and tradition.

■ BACKGROUND

All of us are conscious of the fact that the world consists of a vast number of different cultures. We also recognise that within one particular culture many sub-cultures may exist. Sub-cultures often emphasise values and beliefs which are not stressed in the dominant culture. A complex society may contain within it a range of overlapping cultural identities. It might be useful therefore to perceive culture not as a monolithic phenomenon, but rather as a series of cross-cutting patterns, a matrix or network, where at certain points of reference different cultural identities interact or clash with one another. Culture provides the individual with a way of viewing the world. It becomes social reality. A significant part of a culture's influence resides in its pervasive psychological effects on perceptions, beliefs, values and attitudes. This is true of society and of organisational life.

■ CULTURE AND ORGANISATION

Current interest in the relationship between culture and organisational life can probably be attributed to the extraordinary achievements of the Japanese in the 1970s and the 1980s. Theorists speculated on how such a small country with virtually no natural resources could achieve the highest growth rate, the lowest unemployment rate and come to dominate in one selected industry after another. Most observers would probably agree that Japanese culture has influenced organisational life, but that a major direct influence has been the manner in which Japanese management has structured the culture of individual organisations. As Pascale and Athos (1982) remind us, the 'Art of Japanese Management' has been to achieve an excellent fit between Super-ordinate Goals, Strategy, Structure, Systems, Style, Skills and Staff. These have to be integrated together in corporate cultures that reinforce the beliefs and values of organisations. The aim is to achieve within an organisation a pattern of basic assumptions and shared meaning, which organisational members will use to make sense out of the organisation.

■ CORE ELEMENTS OF CULTURE AND TRADITIONAL LOCAL GOVERNMENT

Most writers on culture would agree that organisational culture can be influenced through:

Environment	Integration
Goals and objectives	History/tradition
Values and beliefs	The people
Differentiation	Transmission
Co-ordination	Rites and rituals

When we reflect on the environment of local government in the 1950s and 60s we consider it to have been a period of consensus politics for local government. Local authorities were seen as providers of services, while also being political institutions with powers for local government. The services provided by local government were mostly prescribed in statute and there was a high degree of consensus in the society about the services local government should provide. While the society wished for public provision it was not involved in any active way in seeking to influence the politics of local government. There was a good degree of consensus among elected councillors from all parties that local government should be a direct provider of professional services to the public. This meant that the administration, as represented by officers, could expect a high degree of acceptance for their suggested implementation strategies.

Local government was differentiated into functional departments with discrete areas of professional activity and at the same time the Centre had developed to perform those functions that were not directly part of service provision. Classically this has meant that separate Legal, Finance and Personnel departments were established. The committee structure largely followed this pattern with elected members gaining their identity from roles on particular committees. This functional structure was a reflection of the growth of professionalism in the society at large and the political structure mirrored the same values.

This system of local government was based on certain goals and objectives. Firstly the idea of self-sufficiency: it was assumed that local government itself should provide the services. This was closely linked to the value society placed on public services: it was deemed appropriate for local government to be a sole provider, in reality having almost a monopoly on public provision. Here we can see the value in the society for public provision affecting local government's own perception and belief. The appropriate structure was interpreted to be functional and hierarchical with central control, thus permitting differentiation and co-ordination as envisaged in the classic bureaucracy. This of course was in perfect keeping with the goals and objectives that society had for a welfare state. A bureaucracy, with its characteristics of a well-defined hierarchy of authority, clear lines of responsibilities, a system of rules and procedures, impersonality of relations and written records, could be expected to administer an impartial service to its citizens. In this way the purpose of local governments could be clearly integrated into the values of the society as a whole. This view was compounded by the value placed on the professionalism of the service. Professionals defined the service that was good for their clients. This generally meant a uniform standardised service delivery approach. Britain had not begun to come to grips with the reality of the cultural diversity within society. The professional was perceived as knowing best what people needed. The public were seen as being uniform in character so that for example the provision by Social Services of 'meals on wheels' made the assumption that everyone ate meat.

As local government departments expanded they became more differentiated in operational services. One of the concerns of the Maud Committee on the Management of Local Government (1967) was the internal organisation of local authorities. The Committee recognised the wide differentiation that had occurred in local government and linked it to the tradition of associating particular committees with particular services, coupled with the statutory requirements for certain services to have specific committees. The committee in fact recommended that local authorities should seek a more integrated approach and put forward proposals in this regard for structural reorganisation.

So when we look at the culture of traditional local government of the 1950s and 60s we can associate it with the following characteristics. It grew in a stable environment of economic growth. It assumed the sole provider role. It adopted a bureaucratic structure based on functional professionalism. Services were delivered in a uniform manner to clients. Local government operated in an environment of consensus politics, with the committee system mirroring that of the administrative structure. All these features were built on a shared value system of a professional impartial service to clients, which in turn reflected the values of the wider social welfare state.

■ THE ORGANISATIONAL CULTURE OF TRADITIONAL LOCAL GOVERNMENT

Charles Handy (1985) has produced a very useful typology describing four different types of organisational culture. In describing four distinct types of culture, Handy is careful to point out that these are pure types which will not really exist in their entirety in one particular organisation. However, an organisation may display more of one particular culture than another. Equally common is a combination of one, two, three or all four existing in different parts of the one organisation. He distinguishes between Role Culture, Power Culture, Task Culture and Person Culture. In the mid-1980s on courses at INLOGOV when I distributed questionnaires asking local government officers to identify the culture of their local authority on average 72 per cent of respondents identified role culture as the dominant one.

Role culture

Role culture is represented in Handy's concept by a Greek temple with tall columns upon which rests a pediment. This organisational culture perceives its strength to rest in its pillars. In local government we immediately think of the separate professional departments, each with a Chief Officer who has risen up through her/his column. The pediment is where co-ordination takes place with a narrow band of senior management, in our case the Chief Officers of the professional departments led by the Chief Executive, who traditionally had been a legal professional. The work and interaction of the pillars/departments are controlled by systems of rules and procedures with clearly defined responsibilities and authority. This culture works on logic and rationality which reinforces the idea of impersonality of relations with clients and promotion based on professional/technical qualification. This pattern can be clearly identified within traditional local government, where one observed chief officers who had risen on professional expertise to be barons of their domain, defending their departments' professional interests. Obviously Handy identifies role culture as being associated with the classic bureaucracy. Traditional local government is indeed in this mould. Professionalism has added further dimensions to the role culture with very powerful individual professional departments seeking to expand and mark out their area of operation. An interesting observation about bureaucracies is that they function best in stable environments where they are asked to handle large uniform, routine, and known tasks. This is precisely what was required of local government in the UK in the 1950s and 60s. Generally we can say that both the hierarchical structure and associated role culture were correct for the climate of certainty and consensus that was then prevalent in local government.

In organisational behavioural terms this kind of culture encourages organisational members to take a very inward-looking perspective. The stable external environment means that organisational members feel secure in their jobs and their roles; certainty and known solutions predominate in the operational environment. Treasurers will fondly remember the practice of predicting the basis for next year's budget to be the same as last year's with an allowance for inflation, to which was then added an element for growth. As the bureaucracy becomes concerned with its own perpetuation the rules that govern service delivery such as uniformity, professional standards and known solutions are mirrored in the terms and conditions of organisational members. So it was with local government; a uniform pay scale, clearly defined job descriptions, clear routes for progression to reflect the concept of a professional career. Organisation and individual performance were judged by professional standards and the ability to spend the exact budgetary allocation. Promotion came to those who demonstrated a steady hand on the wheel. I use this metaphor deliberately because it conjures male images and in senior posts in local government male management was the dominant reality.

Power culture

It would be remiss not to emphasise that while the role culture was undoubtedly dominant, at least one other culture was strongly represented in traditional local government. Power culture is depicted by a spider's web, with a central figure at the core from which spread rays of power and influence. This central figure is connected by functional or specialist strings but the power rings are the centres of activity and influence. This culture works on precedent. Individuals who aspire to promotion, seek to anticipate the wishes and decisions of the central figure. There are few rules and procedures, control being exercised by the centre. It is in essence a political organisation where decisions are largely taken on the balance of influence. It does not necessarily have to be associated with politics, but it describes very well the politics of traditional local government. Here it was quite common for the Leader of the ruling party to bestow the Chairman/Chairwoman role of powerful committees to favoured party members who had anticipated the political direction of Leader and party. This kind of reward incentive sought to ensure the future anticipation of direction by those so chosen and to encourage others to anticipate patronage. It clearly reflects the reality of political life where loyalty to, and promotion of, political belief is a core value. While officers were promoted on professional expertise, elected councillors were promoted within the political system on the basis of political expertise. Both officers and councillors, however, valued and promoted professional knowledge within the service provider role. This consensus permitted officers to anticipate the wishes of councillors, in the form of a strong advisory professional implementation role. There appeared to be a general belief in the concept of a separation between policy and implementation, yet committee agenda often focused on implementation.

In political behaviour terms one needs to appreciate that politicians never had the same degree of certainty about their political career. As they often noted, they put their performance on the line on a regular basis at election time. Politicians were working to much tighter time horizons. In this sense Leaders who sought to promote like-minded councillors, or influencers were strategically seeking to improve the possibility of achieving politically desirable objectives. There is between the two cultures described the potential for culture clash. Officers are approaching policy objectives from a steady state, a known professional perspective, while politicians are conscious of the need to deliver a political manifesto to their electorate. In general terms, however, despite the power of policy-making being in the political domain, in the vast number of traditional local governments it was the role culture which dominated the total organisation. This can be attributed to the value placed by both officers and members on the professional service delivery function and the consensus politics of the society.

In generalised organisational behaviour terms this dominant relationship led to very formal stilted exchanges, where officers and members related to one another from behind stereotypical views of each other. The formal role play of the council chamber was not conducive to developing a deeper understanding of the differing perspective. Of course individual senior members and officers formed good working relationships but the sheer size of the administrative machine weighed heavily against the elected councillor policy momentum. One needs also to take into account that during the 1950s and 60s there was less emphasis on policy; in one sense it was taken for granted.

Task culture

Also present in pockets of traditional local government was the task culture. This culture is represented by a net where each unit is connected to others while being self-contained at the same time. Power lies at the interstices of the net and not necessarily at the top as in role and power culture. The quickest way to appreciate this type of organisation is to imagine a matrix organisation, where everyone is involved in project work. This requires an ability to form and reform project teams according to the requirements of the different tasks within the organisation. A strong value in this culture is expert power rather than position power or personal power. When successful it is essentially a team culture where people strive together to solve problems. Control can be difficult, in the sense that each project team will seek a high level of resourcing to facilitate the best solution. It does best in a resource-rich climate. The culture performs well in a competitive market where speed of reaction, creativity and integration are important factors.

This culture was found in traditional local government within sections of particular departments, but it is was not the dominant culture. Engineer's departments often had project teams which operated in this way.

In traditional local government task culture encounters difficulties when it knocks against the dominant role culture. The classic example is when project teams are formed on the basis of expert knowledge and not seniority. Members of the project teams find they have two bosses, the project team leader and their traditional line manager. This interface calls for delicate negotiation of time allocation, reporting procedures and accountabilities. Project teams tend to believe in the importance of their task, which creates feelings of being influential. This can create problems within a role culture where influence is associated with position power.

Person culture

Handy describes this culture as unusual because the person is the central point in this culture. One may think of a group of individual stars coming together to share business facilities. An example would be a group of solicitors or doctors each with their own speciality and clients. In professional practices of this kind the organisation is subordinate to the individual. The individuals join the organisation to pursue their own career paths. This person culture while not present in local government in the sense of formal professional practices, can be observed in the way individual professionals manage their career paths within local government. For some people the pursuit of career is a dominant feature of their behaviour, a feature which may well be resented by those with whom they work. The fact that each local authority recruits and promotes independently permits considerable voluntary movement between authorities by individual officers seeking new challenges and promotion. Some officers who are known by the title of 'fast trackers' bestow their talents on particular authorities usually for a short space of time while seeking an increased reputation in a high-profile area of operation. The negative view of this approach is that these officers do not necessarily seek to contribute in a holistic way to their authorities but only contribute where there exists clear advantage for themselves. It needs to be acknowledged that often authorities do benefit from the presence of these 'fast trackers'. The issue is that such behaviour is not in keeping with the dominant role culture where promotion comes more slowly and individuals are appreciated for adopting the values of the role culture. Individual stars often wish to challenge the status quo by pursuing their objectives in new ways that they believe will achieve the desired result.

■ CULTURE CHANGE

The combination of central government legislation and a more informed society in the 1980s resulted in local government examining its core values, mode of operations and its aims and objectives. John Stewart (1986) rightly points out that the new values that will emerge to be nourished in local government, will vary from authority to authority. This fact recognises the diversity of local government and the importance of each authority grounding itself in the reality of its own unique local community. Nevertheless one could observe the formulation of two sets of corporate values that were emerging in the public domain. The first has been named the New Public Management (NPM) and is used to describe a set of administrative doctrines which have dominated the public sector agenda in Britain and the OECD countries. The second is the Public Service Orientation advocated by Stewart and Ranson (1988). Most observers and writers have noted the following components as being strongly emphasised and present in developments with management in the public sector:

- Hands-on professional management in the public sector, meaning active visible discretionary control : 'free to manage'
- Explicit standards and measures of performance
- Greater emphasis on output controls. Resource allocation and rewards linked to measured performance: break-up of centralised bureaucracy
- Shift to disaggregation of units in the public sector, break-up of former monolithic units
- Shift to greater competition/privatisation/market testing etc.
- Stress on private sector styles of management practice
- Stress on greater discipline and parsimony in resource use, cutting direct costs

From the above components you can see how the values are emphasised in the following list.

The values of the New Public Management

- Accountability
- Transparency
- Economy
- Efficiency
- Effectiveness
- Responsibility
- Less bureaucracy
- Participation
- Competition
- Management Responsibility

By the mid-1980s there was considerable debate as to whether management in the private sector was distinctive from management in the public sector. Advocates of the distinctive nature of the public sector accepted that specific management ideas could be transferred to the public sector but they doubted that the 'private sector model' could be totally transferred.

Stewart and Ranson (1988) as proponents of the distinctiveness of public sector management put forward the Public Service Orientation with the following key features for managing the public sector.

- The public domain should be viewed as a site for societal learning
- The concept of strategy should be viewed as a set of expressly political purposes which themselves reflect public aspirations as revealed by a process of political debate
- Budgeting, similarly, should be regarded as an exercise in choice determined through political bargaining
- The rationing of public services must be based on an assessment of need
- Value-laden decisions characterise both public and private sector, but the achievement of collective value is the purpose of the public domain
- Public management usually entails interactions with different agencies and organisations
- Performance monitoring is concerned not only with efficiency and effectiveness, but with the unexpected impact, and with values denied
- There is a dilemma in reconciling political control and staff potential
- Public accountability goes beyond the idea of just holding to account. It

requires the public manager to find ways of giving account, in many different forms and at different levels. Caution and propriety must not be allowed to stifle experiment and responsiveness to the public

While the Public Service Orientation (PSO) did appear to be more coherent in terms of the reality and values of the public domain, its proponents pointed to the dilemma that 'neither representative democracy nor participatory democracy sits easily with industrial democracy' (Stewart and Ranson, 1988). For example we can look at a County Education Department organising a public consultation exercise on Principles for Change in Schools. This requires public meetings and discussions in all the potentially affected communities. Education staff can expect to attend evening meetings at least twice a week for three months. This represents an excellent initiative in terms of participatory and representative democracy but we ought to be aware that staff have been required to work extremely long hours with no extra monetary reward. The fact that staff are prepared to work in this fashion is a compliment to commitment but not necessarily industrial democracy. So far no-one, even at the level of theory, has developed a detailed formulation for combining industrial democracy for public service staff, involving participation by customer/citizen in the design, operation and monitoring of services with representative democracy in the shape of traditional elections to produce representatives who will oversee these same services. Perhaps the circle can never be squared. However PSO points to a wider set of values:

Values of the PSO model of management

- Collective choice in the polity
- Need for resources
- Openness for public action
- The equity of need
- The search for justice
- Citizenship
- Collective action as the instrument of the polity
- Voice as the condition

What we can say about PSO is that it focuses on a wider set of objectives and seeks to realise a more extensive range of values. Therefore we would expect more complexity. It is precisely because it addresses the distinctive features of the public services that these problems arise. PSO and the NPM both stress the importance of getting close to the public as consumer as well as a re-establishment of the public-service ethic, but PSO also stresses the public as citizen.

The above describes the two sets of beliefs and ideas which have sought to influence the overall corporate culture of local government in the UK as it is developing in the 1990s. What has been fascinating to observe and record is the creation of this cultural change both in the broad sense and in particular local authorities. The process of culture change is not easy, not least because it will challenge existing strategies, structures and systems or 'the way things are done around here'.

The process of creating a new culture in local authorities

This example is from one local authority but the pattern is general. The first step in the process has been for an authority, represented by the chief officers, to develop an overall strategy. Many but by no means all of these, have been around the strategy of a Public Service Orientation, or Quality Services. Being customer-oriented means ensuring that the services provided are those customers want. It means putting the customer first. It means understanding that the only reason the authority exists is to provide services to the public. We might like to compare this to the Japanese tradition of super-ordinate goals. This takes the form of a statement of purpose that is then translated into Authority-wide core values. These core values are intended to inform the policies and practices of the whole organisation. In keeping with the Public Service Orientation strategy, here is an example of core values from a district council:

Our Core Values are:

- We are customer-oriented
- We believe in the abilities of the individual
- We must be responsive and responsible
- We believe in quality
- We are action-oriented

The setting of the overall strategic goal and core values for the authority has typically taken place at the corporate level of the authority, usually by chief officers and members finding ways to work together or in parallel to work out the strategy. The strategy and core values are then passed down to each department by their respective chief officers, and each department then formulates a departmental approach to service delivery on the basis of the strategic goal and core values. This process is repeated within sub-sections of all departments so that all staff may begin to 'behave the culture'. If we continue with the public service example, the intention is that each individual's job is specified in terms of the Core Values.

See the boxed example below for how Core Values finally impact on the Main Switchboard Telephonist's role.

Customer-oriented

Over 70 per cent of initial contacts with the Council begin on the telephone and your role in creating an initial impression is absolutely crucial. In fact, the importance of the telephonist's role in ensuring that we are customer-oriented from the beginning cannot be over-stressed.

The basic ground rules in dealing with incoming calls are agreed as follows:

i   Give a clear and friendly greeting, i.e.Good morning/afternoon, (name of council)

ii Reassure waiting callers where appropriate that they are not forgotten.

iii Be helpful and friendly at all times because the caller is relying on you.

Responsive and responsible

It means answering incoming calls as quickly as possible, and making sure that we know **exactly** what the caller wants and putting them through to the right extension. Listen carefully to what the caller has to say, be responsive and show respect to the customer. Your voice is the human factor of the organisation and the way you treat individual callers will affect the way in which the council is seen. You are the council as far as the caller is concerned. Remember that each of us is responsible for presenting the image of the council as efficient, friendly and helpful.

Belief in the abilities of the individual

This means that the council has confidence in you to do your job by providing the necessary support, encouragement, facilities and training to help you. Performance Appraisal is part of this process.

Action-oriented – getting jobs done

It means:

i   Ensuring the telephone procedure on the main switchboard is a credit to the organisation.

ii Establishing consistency in the way the telephone is answered.

iii Keeping the telephonist's directory up to date with new starters and leavers.

iv When taking telephone messages for someone, making sure that the message is dealt with.

v   Knowing all departments and their functions so that help can be given immediately to a vague enquirer and they can be put through to the right person.

Belief in quality and quality control

This means that we aim to impress and demonstrate to our customers the quality of our telephone practices and techniques. We will **not** opt for second best.

In assessing whether the organisation has a good telephone practice and technique, the customer will ask the following questions.

1 Was my call answered promptly?

2 Was I answered in a friendly and courteous manner?

3 Did I have to wait long before I was connected?

4 Was I connected to the right person/department?

5 Was I passed from pillar to post?

6 Did I feel it was frustrating to deal with the Council by telephone or did I find it a pleasure?

The aim is to ensure that the customer finds it a pleasure to deal with the council every time he has occasion to telephone. Your role in this is vital.

This boxed example demonstrates how the organisation seeks to inculcate the culture into the job behaviour of the individual. The aim is to achieve through a series of meetings between numbers of staff a translation of the culture from broad strategic goals into departmental, group and individual aims and objectives. Having clearly stated how the strategy and core values will affect organisational and individual delivery of services, the question remains, what structural and systemic changes need to be considered to support the cultural change?

■ CULTURAL ANALYSIS OF THE CHANGES WITHIN LOCAL GOVERNMENT

Fragmentation and behaviour

We have noted that the predominant culture of local government has been role culture, with the other cultures also present in the environment. Handy would suggest that an organisation should differentiate its cultures and structures according to the dominant activity in each department, division or section. The new management of local government recognises the diversity within the environment and seeks innovative ways of providing services. We can appreciate that known, routine, steady state tasks can be handled in a culture where rules, procedures, controls and regulations facilitate fast processing. The handling of rent and rebate payments in a housing department would be an example. Economic development on the other hand, with its need to enter into partnerships with other agencies often on a project-by-project basis, is better suited to a task culture, where the emphasis is on finding speedy and flexible solutions. The skill therefore is to recognise the diversity of tasks that local government is engaged in and to structure the authority accordingly. This has in fact begun to occur in response to the challenges of the 1990s. Some authorities, in their pursuit of cultural change, have broken up their large central departments and replaced them with a small strategic core, with professional support services being created to supply services to the service departments on a commercial basis. Lincolnshire and Northamptonshire display this approach. Other authorities, including Lincolnshire, have created internal markets with an emphasis on profit centres, cost centres and business units responsible for discrete elements of service. This has also meant putting support services like personnel and legal, for example, on a business footing.

The breaking down of the monolithic departments into discrete units has meant that within these units we increasingly find a culture that is task-oriented with a greater emphasis on a team approach. Culture clash can occur between the new units and their core department if the core is still strongly operating from a role perspective. This clash can be mirrored again between the core of service departments and the core of the authority when it is seeking to ensure corporate action across the authority as a whole.

Staff who operate in these newer units display many changed patterns of behaviour. Here are a few that you will recognise:

- a sense of urgency: a need to have a response immediately
- a feeling of threat: only they are exposed
- a positive expression of enjoying the pace and 'being out in the real world'
- a feeling of pride in the unit achievements
- a frustration with the parent department or the core of the authority
- an obsession with costs, quality and customers
- a feeling of isolation
- a concern that other units are not operating according to the same rules

Staff in the core of the authority display some of these behavioural patterns:

- an awareness of being part of a new, leaner core, and consequent support for the service emphasis
- a concentration on strategic direction, characterised by the need to communicate it across the authority
- a concern that fragmentation means loss of overall objectives
- a feeling of defensiveness about the costs of the core
- an inability really to understand the emphasis on costs
- an obsession with providing a quality service to the operational units
- a wish to be appreciated
- a concern with probity
- a concern with corporate values
- a concern for the authority to operate in particular areas as one organisation

Staff in core service departments display some of the following behaviours:

- a concern with departmental objectives and values
- a concern with policy initiatives and guidelines
- a concern for monitoring and evaluation of the operational units
- a wish to maintain a distance from the core of the authority
- a wish to decide for themselves when to co-operate and when to compete

- a pride in their operational units
- an obsession with providing support to their operational units

The above lists demonstrate some of the diversity of organisational behavioural responses to the changing environment of local authorities.

Political interface

In local government policy is the domain of the elected councillors. Handy believes that policy decisions operate best in a power culture, which is exactly how the politics of local government works. The changes that have taken place have, of course, affected the way politicians and officers interact. For example decentralisation has meant that officers lower in the hierarchy have increased contact with members.

The following two quotations from David Blunkett, as Leader of Sheffield City Council in 1980, and Michael Spungin, a County Councillor from Nottinghamshire in 1985, when discussing relationships between officers and members illustrate the changes.

David Blunkett, 1980

'it is very difficult to have a clear-cut idea that here are two separate groups, the politicians who get on with the formulation and direction of policy and officers who are aloof from this who have nothing to do with the political arena and actually get on with implementation. And both officers and members know that this isn't true; that officers are inherently involved in the formulation of policy because of the nature of information giving that they are deeply involved in, and that members are involved in carrying those policies out. And they have got to be because changing policies is about knowing whether they're working and being able to monitor and evaluate the success of what's taking place, and getting feedback from those who, after all, are supposed to be the beneficiaries, those in the community.

So it's a very mixed up situation and its at least worth being honest about it and accepting that, and saying we do need reasonable lines of communication that enable us to stop officers being totally sucked into party political struggle but accept that the political nature of their work is recognised and with Members that they don't actually take over as managers of the service although some of us would be very happy to have their salaries'

Michael Spungin, County Councillor, on the new kind of officer:
Someone who would have risen to the top in any business he came to choose because he has got the intelligence to recognise the more delicate touches and also someone who is prepared to be--- I won't say 'rubber like' but certainly sufficiently resilient to bend with whatever political climate he's faced with. The political complexion of authorities has changed in places where changes were never ever anticipated and officers who imagined that they would be able to conduct themselves in one manner or been allowed to think in one direction are having to face something entirely new.

The problem is this. The councillors the officers are dealing with contain among them a new breed of those who are not only politically committed but are determined to do more than just lay down policy guidelines. Many of them, and I'm talking on both sides of politics, the left and the right, are determined to see the particular policies to which they are committed implemented in detail and they will be involved in progress chasing, right down to the details of administration, sometimes further than I might say, was appropriate (September 1985).

There is no doubting the re-assertion of the power culture in the form of clear political will in many local authorities in the 1980s. This transition, in a minority of cases, led to marked turbulence with sometimes negative effects for the effectiveness of services. The much more positive outcome was that the majority of councils found innovative ways for officers and Members working together to meet the needs of local communities. This can be seen in newly formed local area committees, member involvement in performance review panels, community development funds, consumer panels, increased officer support for the democratic process.

In organisational behavioural terms this has meant that many more officers and members communicate with one another in terms of relating to each other as individuals, rather than through some stereotypical role. Officers demonstrate a clearer understanding of the political context of individual members and seek to be informed of the realities of members' 'patches'. Equally members have appreciated the value of working constructively with officers to ensure effective outcomes for citizens. This has increased the opportunity for enhanced policy implementation. This is not to imply that all is perfection. There are also many instances of the failure of dialogue in this vital relationship.

Patterns of recruitment

The person culture can be seen to contribute through individual stars being recruited to bestow their talents on particular local governments. This trend is apparent in the recruitment of private sector expertise for the specialist Direct Service Organisations brought about as a result of Compulsory Competitive Tendering. It is also seen in the recruitment of Chief Executives on short-term contracts at a high salary to undertake a specific task for an authority. The main point I want to highlight here is what happens to the person who moves across cultures, from private to public for example, or from one authority to another. This will often depend on the cultural sensitivity of the newcomers and the degree of perception they display to their new environment. We could of course leave it at that and many authorities do. We often hear the stories of the new Chief Officer or Chief Executive who wants to reorganise on the basis of what worked in her/his old authority. From a management perspective this is very wasteful for the new authority. It is much more productive to arrange a programme at the appropriate level for the new incumbent through which the complexities of the organisational culture can be revealed, but it still depends upon his/her recognition of the need to learn.

The introduction of new high profile posts can increase pressures on the newcomers to perform, once the mandatory honeymoon period is over. It is of course equally tempting for the senior staff whom they join to sit back and watch the action — 'Let them sort it out' kind of syndrome or, even more destructive, work covertly against any changes from the strong position of knowing the authority or department better than the newcomer.

Systems

Those authorities engaged in cultural change realised the need to adapt their systems to support the core values espoused in their culture. This often meant a significant increase in the training budget so that staff could be given the skills to perform in the new manner. Performance appraisal also had to operate to support the goals of the organisation, therefore targets had to reflect the new focus. This meant targets were output-oriented and measured in terms of quantity and quality. Priorities were reflected in the budget allocation with bids being made on an output basis. Management information systems had to change to provide the service delivery departments and their operational units, with information in a form that is useful for them and not one that is best suited for central requirements. Management has to be seen to be behaving the culture itself, and this is true for management as a whole as well as for individual managers.

■ CONCLUSIONS

Local authorities have recognised the different cultures that exist within one organisation. Therefore they have sought to use the concept of corporate culture to assist the organisation in external adaptation and internal integration. In so doing they have focused on the following elements of culture to ensure survival and adaptation:

- core values
- core mission
- core goals and objectives which inform the development of all other goals and objectives
- the development of the means to attain the goals such as organisational structure, management resource systems and training programmes
- the development of performance review systems
- the development of a common language across operational areas

While many Chief Executives and Chief Officers have been aware of the need to act the new culture this has been harder to sustain on an authority-wide basis. We know of the stories of Chief Executives spending the day on the front desk to emphasise getting close to the customer. The problem is how to maintain that kind of symbolism so that it becomes grounded in everyday organisational reality. One way is to reward behaviour in keeping with the culture in a clear up-front manner, thus creating many role models. For success the culture must make clear where the power lies and how individuals may be rewarded or punished.

■ IMPLICATIONS FOR YOU AS MANAGER

This chapter has shown how local government is part of the cultural matrix, making and developing its own collective adjustments to the situation in which it finds itself. In this sense culture is a human product subject to change over time and place. Managers wishing to understand the cultural context of organisational behaviour need to look to the core elements of culture: environment, goals and objectives, values and beliefs, differentiation, co-ordination, integration, history/tradition, the people, transmission and rites and rituals to begin to appreciate the organisational reality. Handy's typology was used to look at the culture of traditional local government and show how different cultures can co-exist, clash or dominate within the one organisation. The chapter emphasised the important role values play in formulating or reformulating a culture, and how the concept of corporate culture is used to integrate individuals and differentiated departments to operate towards common goals.

References

Handy, C. (1985) *Gods of Management.* Pan Business, London

Hood, C. (1991) 'A public management for all seasons?', *Public Administration* (69:1, Spring, pp.3–19)

The Maud Committee Report on the Management of Local Government (1967) HMSO, London

Stewart, J. (1986) *The New Management of Local Government.* Allen & Unwin, London

Stewart, J. and Ranson, S. (1988) 'Management in the public domain', *Public money and Management* 8 (2) Spring–Summer, 13–19

Pascale, R.T. and Athos, A.G. (1982) *The Art of Japanese Management.* Allen Lane, London

2

Understanding myself as a manager

Key points

◆ An effective manager needs to understand the context in which managerial tasks take place and the interpersonal relationship elements which affect the manner in which people undertake tasks.

◆ The context of local government requires managers to understand party politics and organisational politics. Managers differ in their ability to manage this complex political environment.

◆ Skills in political sensitivity often denote the effective manager.

◆ An effective manager understands that the outcome of managerial tasks can be influenced by the context of situations and her/his own individual values and beliefs.

◆ A pro-active model of individual political skills outlines the importance of reading situations and understanding what we as individuals bring to particular situations. it is offered as a framework to assist managers in enhancing their political sensitivity.

■ INTRODUCTION

It is accepted wisdom that before you can manage others, you ought to be able to manage yourself. This instinctively sounds sensible and therefore meets with general approval. The problem is; what do we mean by manage. If it is the classic definition of management which includes planning, organising, co-ordinating, controlling, reviewing and ordering, it is only half of the picture. The emphasis is on the rational task requirements of the job, but people are both social and emotional and these factors effect their behaviour. Managers, to be more effective, need to understand themselves in relation to both their work context, organisational culture being one example of context, and their work colleagues. This means understanding the content and process elements of situations.

This chapter offers a framework for analysing individual organisational behaviour which focuses on two dimensions. The manager's degree of awareness and sensitivity to the organisational environment, which is related to an ability to read particular situations; and the degree to which the manager takes account of self and others, which is related to our individual socialisation processes. This pro-active model of individual managerial behaviour suggests an interesting typology of behaviours namely; clever, wise, inept and naive. This is used to explore the benefits of achieving one's own goals and those of others.

■ THE DISTINCTION BETWEEN 'CONTENT' AND 'PROCESS'

It is easiest to think of **content** as a specific area of knowledge such as knowing the individual elements required to devise a business plan or a marketing strategy. **Process** on the other hand is the behavioural skills required to gain acceptance by others of your business plan or marketing strategy. An example will illustrate the point more clearly. In the early days of community care I was visiting a county council who were determined to be prepared for the purchaser/provider split. The County Social Services Department had set in motion a rigorous timetable when all business plans were to be completed and submitted. This resulted in several area managers devising business plans without consulting their management teams. The county met its planning deadline for business plans, but several area managers were having difficulty gaining acceptance within their management teams for their business plans. The content of the business plans may have been exactly executed but the process issues had been forgotten.

If we consider the recent changes in local government we can see the tendency to concentrate our responses on the content requirements of these changes. Local government officers are becoming competent at business planning, marketing strategies, service levels agreements and cost centre management, to name but a few. However, the process issues are just as important. In fact it is the combination of content and process when applied to particular situations that leads to effective performance by the individual.

Some local authorities are working on the process issues. Here are three examples of what this approach focuses on:

Setting purpose and direction

The manager takes a helicopter view; demonstrates foresight and judgement; is good in advocacy role; handles representative and policy roles with confidence; knows how to persuade and influence; is diplomatic and confident; appreciates when to be flexible.

Interpersonal skills

The manager understands others' point of view; is able to depersonalise comments and criticisms; has good listening skills; is consultative, resilient and optimistic; demonstrates fairness and sensitivity; is responsive, caring and receptive; can tolerate ambiguity more than one right way; has good self-management.

Political sensitivity

The manager understands how own values influence interpretations; reads the external and internal environments; considers all the stakeholders; is a good networker; maintains own integrity; looks for opportunities to collaborate; shows awareness of organisational culture and power.

Lists such as the above emphasise person-related sets of behaviour (process skills) that a person must display in order to perform the tasks and functions of his/her job (content skills).

■ APPROACHES TO ORGANISATIONAL BEHAVIOUR

Historically managers thought there was only one way to manage people because organisations and managerial tasks were similar to the relationship between managers and employees in management production industry. This led to a **prescriptive approach to management.** The approach emphasised organising tasks in such a way that efficiency could be maximised. We often associate it with a time and motion approach to tasks. Find the best way to perform the task, implement that as a routine and ensure it is followed by a process of rewards and punishment for performance and output. We like to think that we have seen this as too simplistic an approach. Nevertheless it still survives in local government, often in managerial attitude to juniors. Anyone who has visited Macdonalds can see this approach in action, from the prescribed production process to the mechanistic service delivery. If we wanted to be unkind to local government and Treasurers in particular we could find this approach in some payroll sections.

It was Elton Mayo of Harvard University who clearly demonstrated the importance that group structure and environmental conditions had on the individual performance of group members. In essence these studies showed that individuals are complex beings and not just ergonomic production units. The work of Mayo and his colleagues, commonly referred to as the Hawthorne Studies, led to an awareness of the importance of a **human relations approach to management.** Managers could improve performance by adopting participative approaches rather than autocratic approaches and by giving attention to the group dynamics of work settings.

In keeping with the concept of individuals being complex bundles of physical and intellectual properties it follows most naturally that organisations themselves are multi-faceted systems. The systems approach to organisations recognises the interrelationships between the parts of the organisation. It asks us to consider the validity of interpreting a part of a system only in relation to the whole system. This is something with which local government has to struggle: Departments/Managers often wish to interpret events only from a departmental perspective. When we begin to look at things in a holistic manner it brings a different understanding of organisational behaviour. A systems approach to organisational behaviour encourages us to consider complex cause and effect relationships between a range of factors which include demographic forces, cultural forces, political forces, economic forces, technological forces and competitive forces. In short the individual behaviour that a person exhibits is the result of the interrelationships and interdependencies of sub-systems within the whole system.

Another useful approach to understanding organisational behaviour is the contingency approach. This theory rejects the idea of universal principles being applied to managing behaviour in organisations. Contingency theory suggests that the best management responses are decided by examining the characteristics of particular situations. The art of successful management is the ability to diagnose a situation correctly. You will see that the model I am about to introduce has been influenced by the human relations, systems and contingency approach to organisational behaviour.

■ A MODEL OF INDIVIDUAL ORGANISATIONAL BEHAVIOUR FOR A POLITICAL ENVIRONMENT

Rationale for the model

The model was devised some years ago by myself with three other academic psychologists, Tanya Arroba, Simon Baddeley and Kim James, when we were all colleagues at the Institute for Local Government Studies at the University of Birmingham. Our starting point was that within local government:

- managers had to manage 'small p' and 'large P' politics

- managers differed in their ability to manage different political situations

- organisational politics could be viewed as an organisational attempt to overcome the inherent internal contradictions or

- organisational politics is behaviour unrequired or undesired by the organisation and designed to pursue the self interest of individuals or subunits.

The literature on organisational politics, which gained momentum again in the 1980s (see Kakabadse, 1983; Lee and Lawrence, 1985), and local government officers themselves express both positive and negative views about the nature of organisational politics. Organisational politics as used here, refers to the outcome of the interrelationships of organisational members with organisational design. The activity is instrumental in character and may have positive or negative results for individual, group and organisational goals. Political behaviour is seen as an influence process, participation by the individual or group means that, dependent on the situation, differing resources will be called upon. These resources include power, status, individual attributes (e.g. intelligence, knowledge) personal relationships, material resources and human resources. Whether the political behaviour will be perceived as legitimate will depend on a) the behaviour being in pursuit of sanctioned organisational goals or sanctioned informal norms; b) the attributions of the observers. This kind of organisational politics needs to be distinguished from party politics. Seeking to outline a composite view we can say that both organisational political behaviour and party political behaviour are present in local government. This is one of the distinguishing features of management in local government, the ability of managers to manage 'small p' (organisational politics) and 'large P' (party politics).

Many writers have emphasised the importance of understanding politics at work. Kakabadse (1983) suggests that understanding this area can enable a manager to move beyond the Peter Principle according to which sooner or later an individual rises to the level of her/his own incompetence. It was a realisation that individuals differed in their political sensitivity that prompted us to develop a model of individual political behaviour. The purpose of the model would be to facilitate consideration of the skills needed to manage organisational politics. Underpinning this thrust was a firm belief in the capacity of the individual to acquire new skills once the awareness of their importance and significance had been validated. The introduction to the model will bring clarification to the discussion.

A model of political skills

This is a pro-active model which looks at individual political action and describes four patterns of behaviour which each individual has in their repertoire. It recognises that an individual may band between the four patterns of behaviour described. The model is skill-based; it is offered as a method by which managers may reflect on their organisational behaviour. This may lead to an improvement or a fine-tuning of their political skills. The model pays particular attention to two important aspects of the person, cognition and experience.

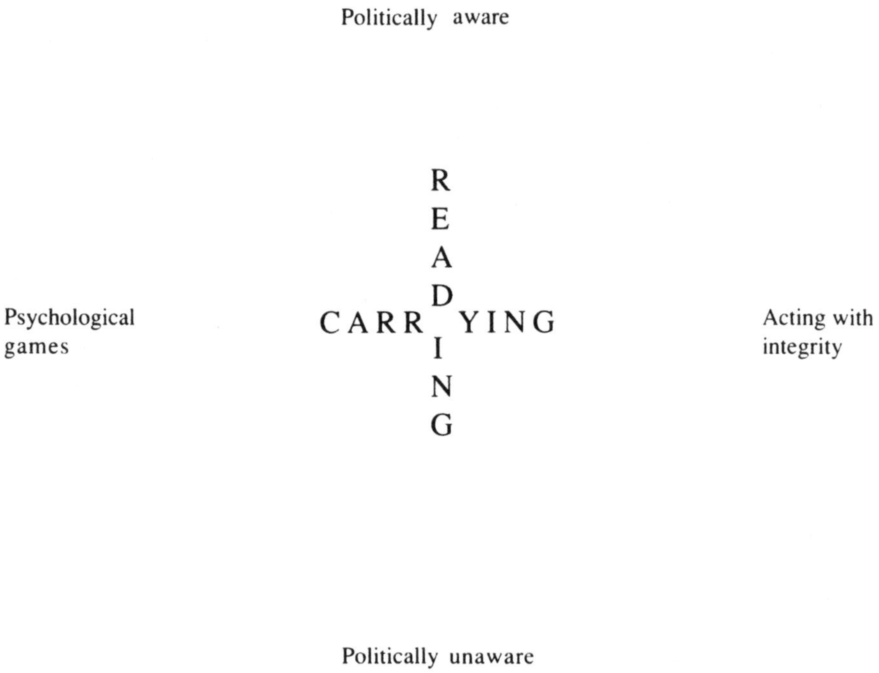

Politically aware

<pre>
                            R
                            E
                            A
                            D
Psychological   C A R R   Y I N G   Acting with
games   I   integrity
                            N
                            G
</pre>

Politically unaware

Figure 2.1

In Figure 2.1 above, the vertical axis represents the dimension of 'Reading' with 'Politically aware' at one end of the pole and 'Politically unaware' at the opposite end. 'Reading' refers to the individual's ability to understand the organisational environment. An individual who is literate in this sense will be aware of the following elements:

- organisational culture
- overt and covert agenda
- decision-making processes
- location of power within and outside the organisation
- political purpose and direction
- 'small p' and 'large P' politics
- clear knowledge of one's own bases of power and influence

Political awareness is seen as involving a recognition of the importance of these factors in particular situations, while being politically unaware implies an inability or unwillingness to take account of these factors.

The horizontal axis represents the dimension of 'Carrying' with psychological game playing at one end of the continuum and acting with integrity at the polar opposite. Carrying refers to the beliefs and values an individual develops over time and experience. This is commonly referred to as our socialisation process. These experiences influence our perceptions and tend to predispose us to act in certain ways. Psychological game playing is the predisposition to maximise one's own needs and wants often to the detriment of both the organisation as a whole, and other people. Psychological games can engender 'bad' feelings based on a preconceived notion of the world. Acting with integrity incorporates an acceptance of self and consideration of others on human terms, reflected in direct and open communication. The dimension of 'Carrying' is clearly influenced by Dr Eric Berne's theory of Transactional Analysis. The theory proposes that individuals, as a consequence of their socialisation process, carry with them a disposition to behave in a certain way in specific situations. Berne categorises social interactions as follows: procedures; pastimes; operations and games.

Berne (1964) gives the following definition of a game:

> A game is an ongoing series of complementary ulterior transactions progressing to a well defined, predictable outcome. Descriptively, it is a recurring set of transactions, often repetitious, superficially plausible, with a concealed motivation
>
> (Berne, p. 44)

When one considers the possibilities for social interaction within an organisation such as local government and the potential for conflict of interest, transactional analysis, when combined with the 'reading dimension', can suggest reasons why individuals behave differently, interpret situations differently, resulting in people having varying degrees of sensitivity to organisational politics.

So we have two axes representing the dimensions 'Reading' and 'Carrying'; even though they are represented graphically as at right angles to each other we should interpret the broken arrows as representing an awareness that what an individual 'reads' will affect what they 'carry' to a situation and vice versa. The model suggests that due to the complexity of behaviour each of us is capable of a variety of responses. They are characterised as Innocent; Wise; Clever and Inept. A person may display each of these behavioural responses dependent on what the manager is 'carrying' and 'reading' in the particular situation. Therefore, no one is all wise, all clever, all innocent , all inept, all of the time. The model defines these behavioural responses so that you the manager may make a pro-active choice about behaviour.

The following case study is used as the base from which to explain and develop the model. You are asked to imagine the Assistant Director responding in the four different response behaviours of Innocent, Wise, Clever and Inept. As each response behaviour is considered the appropriate space will be filled as shown in Figures 2.2, 2.3, 2.4 and 2.5.

A City Council has operated an equal opportunity policy for fifteen years. Recently the Core Personnel Department at the centre of the authority noted through its monitoring and review function that despite the recruitment and selection policies of the Council, personnel who fall into these categories are not advancing to senior positions within the authority. In an effort to encourage Senior and Middle managers to be more aware of how they consciously or unconsciously discriminate in the areas of recruitment, selection and promotion, the core personnel department organised a series of one-day seminars on these issues for managers with responsibilities in these areas. It was felt that this would help to overcome some perceived problems with the personnel functions now being devolved to individual departments, thus making it more difficult to ensure uniform application of the codes of practice. The seminars were well received and attended. The general feedback to the Core Personnel Department was positive and the Chief Executive was pleased with the balance and fairness with which the issues were presented.

Some months later, due to an internal reorganisation and consultation with the unions the opportunity to make an internal promotion arises in the Planning and Transport Department. The promotion is to Group Manager (Strategy and Development) in the division headed by the Assistant Director Strategy and Economic Development. There are six group managers in this division: all sit on the Divisional Management

Cont'd

Team, with the Assistant Director who heads the Division, all are male.There are two candidates for the position of Group Manager (Strategy and Development). Here is a brief work résumé for both:

Tom, aged 37 years.
Section Head (Research), one of the three Section Heads in Strategy and Development where the vacancy arises. Tom has held this post for seven years.
Tom did a five-year degree at University finishing with an M.Sc. in Planning. He also holds the MRTPI.
Tom joined the City Council straight from university and has worked his way up through the department.
He has a good open management style, is liked by his staff and colleagues and obviously enjoys his work. Tom likes living in the area and is happy with the council.

Sue, aged 39 years.
Section Head (Geographical Information System), one of three Section Heads in Information Management and Research.
Sue has a B.Sc. in Computer Science and an M.Sc. in Planning.
Sue went to Canada after university and worked with the Canadian Ordnance Survey for two years. On returning to the UK, she joined a county council and worked on structure plans for three years. Sue then joined IBM to develop in-project management, specifically to work on developing Geographical Information Systems. She joined the City Council five years ago as Section Head.
Sue is well respected by her staff and together they run an effective section. She is interested in a career move.

Below is a presentation of the four behavioural response patterns, Innocent, Wise, Clever and Inept.

Innocent Response: If the Assistant Director responds in an innocent way the behaviour will be concerned with fairness, sticking to the rules with an emphasis on data and facts. Communication will be open and trusting, with little attention to the possibility of hidden agenda. When political behaviour is in the environment it is avoided totally or at best viewed as a compromise. This means that innocent behaviour is located at the 'politically unaware' end of the 'Reading' axis and at the 'acting with integrity' end of the 'Carrying' axis. Topics like equal opportunities would ring lots of alarm bells for the individual who has a tendency to place importance on formal structures, facts and official hierarchies. Value is often placed on neutrality as a means of not reading political issues. You might imagine hearing these comments from Innocent: 'We are fair here, I don't know of ever excluding anyone from promotion because she was a woman. I won't approve of that at all.', or 'Women don't like to take too much responsibility, they are very good though.'

Innocent behaviour will consider others so that the implications of the appointment in terms of feelings and disappointment will be taken account of. The decision is likely to be reached by close adherence to past practice. This means we define Innocent behaviour as occupying the space between political unawareness and acting with integrity (see figure 2.2).

Wise response: Now reflect on the Assistant Director who responds in a wise way. Wise behaviour is associated first and foremost with a multi-dimensional perspective. There is a clear awareness of the possibility of overt and covert agendas, together with an ability to perceive whether current 'flavour of the month' issues are going to be incorporated into new policy guidelines. So, in the example, the wise response would include discovering why the Personnel Department instituted a seminar on equal opportunities, and what were the details of the internal trends, where did Planning and Transport stand in relation to other departments. The higher profile of equal opportunities would be assessed to judge whether the pressure was coming

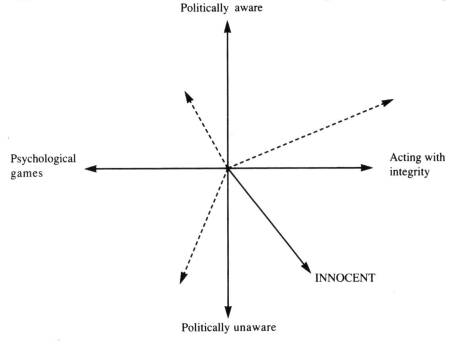

Figure 2.2

from internal or external factors. Wise behaviour will of course consider the ability of the candidates to do the job, but will also go beyond the data and past practice. The implications of appointing Sue if she is the best candidate would be taken account of. Perhaps, as the only woman on the Management Team, she would need initial support in finding her way. Equally it might be that the Management Team would need to evaluate its present way of operating. These would be initial thoughts, not definite preconceptions, just items needing to be considered. This kind of response reflects behaviour towards the 'acting with integrity' end of the 'Carrying' dimension. Wise behaviour comes very much from the adult ego state where there is acceptance of one's own and others' worth. The skill is in achieving one's own goals and assisting others to achieve theirs. The 'Reading' dimension will affect an awareness of the climate of the organisation in its totality and where power and influence are located. Support for initiatives is sought before, not after implementation. Therefore wise behaviour is seen as occupying the space between 'politically aware' and 'acting with integrity' (see Figure 2.3).

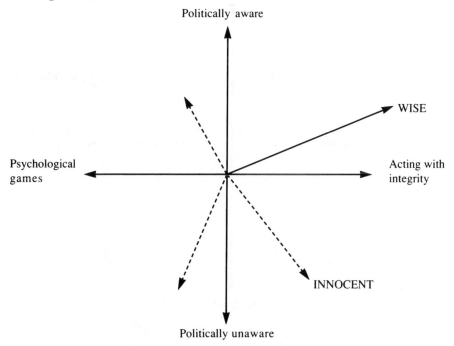

Figure 2.3

Clever behaviour: The Assistant Director who uses clever behaviour also displays a multi-dimensional perspective. What distinguishes it from wise behaviour is the tendency to seek to win irrespective of the cost to others.

This places the response at the psychological game playing end of the 'Carrying' axis. The clever strategy is 'politically aware' on the 'Reading' dimension. The significance of the Personnel Department's initiative will be thoroughly investigated, looking for internal and external trends. If the assessment is made that the new initiative reflects a serious attempt to make policy a reality then Sue would be appointed if she was capable and the best candidate. However, clever behaviour would be likely to appoint Sue without giving any consideration to how the management team and Sue herself would manage the change. Any perceived problems that might arise would be dealt with on the basis of powerful behaviour (I quote 'Let me sort it out, I know things are difficult', the message being, 'I can cope but you can't'.) This reflects a desire to win all the time, the response puts the other person down. This tendency can be displayed when we are feeling defensive. So we place clever behaviour in the space between political awareness and playing psychological games (see Figure 2.4).

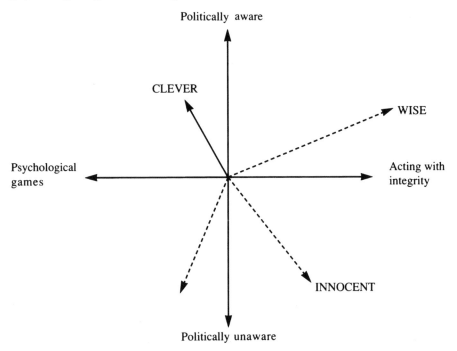

Figure 2.4

Inept behaviour: So we come to the last space in our model, the area for inept behaviour. The distinguishing feature of inept behaviour is the tendency to play psychological games which confirm a poor image of self and others in particular circumstances. There is a lack of ability to read political agenda in relation to the position from which others make proposals. So the inept response would quickly choose Sue for the job, the rationale being as follows: 'Well, we know the way the wind is blowing lets give them an equal opportunities candidate.' The other members in the department would be expected to accept the decision on the basis that they are making the same interpretation of the situation. Inept behaviour recognises that there are power relationships and likes to be associated with them. The strategy tends to be unsuccessful because of a tendency to underestimate own self in particular situations, as well as the complexity and capability of others. So we fill in the last space in the quadrant (see Figure 2.5).

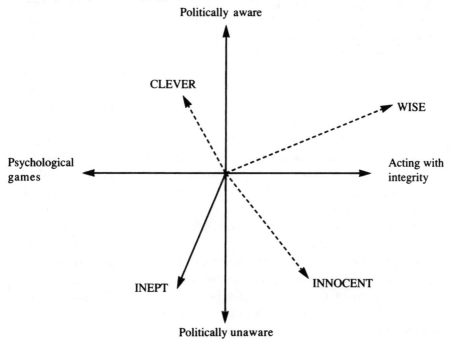

Figure 2.5

The model recognises that each of us is capable of a wide range of behaviours, sometimes Innocent, Wise, Clever and Inept. It seeks to emphasise the reality of an influence process that is multi-dimensional. The manager who wishes to be successful in the sense of achieving targets, planning strategies, introducing change, monitoring trends or making long-term predictions cannot afford to ignore the presence of organisational politics. Wise political behaviour is depicted as the ability to achieve personal and others'/organisational goals while maintaining integrity. This clearly is evaluative in the sense that it seeks to move away from the idea of organisational politics being a negative thing. There is a rejection of organisational politics being a Machiavellian process. The prime purpose of the model is to offer you, the manager, the framework to reflect on your own behavioural tendencies in particular situations and the implication of them for your own and others' success. The essence of the model is how the 'Reading and Carrying' dimensions interact to influence one's own perceptions of issues and outcomes. See below for an amusing illustration of this point:

The Gate-Keeper Story — a Tale of Pre-Assumptions

A local authority had completed a review of its property management with a view to achieving more cost-effective use of buildings. This resulted in some departments sharing accommodation with other departments where once there had been single departmental occupancy. So it transpired that Social Services now had as tenants the Community Services Division of Education. The terms and conditions were worked out with Property Services at Chief officer level and the relocation was completed.

A problem arose in the first week when the Social Services Caretaker asked some members of the Community Services Division to leave the building at 6.30. In fact the caretaker insisted that they left. It transpired that it was the custom for all occupants to be gone by 6.30 so that the caretaker could secure the building. The reading of the situation by the Community Services Manager was that the caretaker should be instructed to accommodate to the working pattern of the new occupants. This view was brought to the discussions with Social Services and Property Services. However the caretaker had a job description and in addition he had accumulated a lot of personal credits with staff in Social Services. He had a reputation for being pleasant and helpful to staff and clients and very willing to go the extra mile. The representatives of Social Services and Property Services could not see why Community Division could not conform to the established norm. This type of situation is difficult to anticipate if an individual permits her or his carrying and reading dimensions to be dominated by pre-set assumptions. The caretaker is still securing the building at 6.30 p.m.

■ IMPLICATIONS FOR YOU AS A MANAGER

This model may be used by you to undertake a degree of self-exploration. It is a useful exercise to reflect back over past organisational situations and consider whether some of the outcomes can be attributed to Innocent, Wise, Clever or Inept behaviour on your part. When we are being entirely honest with ourselves we quietly admit that as Managers our behaviours are strongly influenced by our values, beliefs, individual experiences and the perceived or known demands placed on us by others, a classic example of the latter being departmentalism in local government. Wherever you sit as a manager in local government you are required to manage downwards, upwards and across structural boundaries. You as a manager are seeking to consider the interaction between the formal structure, the tasks to be undertaken, the methods used to undertake the task, your own behaviour and the behaviour of other people, the process of management, the informal structure and the external environment.

Here are some questions for you to consider:

◇ How do you balance your own needs, the needs of others and the needs of the organisation?

◇ Do you structure the working environment in your area of control so that individuals may grow and develop as well as achieving organisational goals?

◇ Are you a content manager i.e. more task focused or are you a process manager i.e. more people focused.?

◇ How aware are you of the effects of the formal structure on your own organisational behaviour?

◇ How much do you allow group pressure to influence your managerial behaviour?

◇ How flexible are you when you discover that others have interpreted a specific situation differently than you?

◇ Are you aware of the values you are using when you make judgements about people and tasks?

◇ How much time do you spend considering how to communicate with members, superiors, peers, subordinates, the public, communities, clients, customers?

◇ How good are you at sharing power, information, knowledge?

◇ Do people work for you or with you?

◇ Are you honest and fair with yourself?

References

Berne, E. (1964) *Games People Play.* Grove Press, New York

Lee, R. and Lawrence, P. (1985) *Organisational Behaviour: Politics at Work.* Hutchinson, London

Kakabadse, A. (1983) *The Politics of Management.* Gower Publishing Co Ltd, Aldershot

3

The importance of group processes

> **Key points:**
> ♦ *The changes in the working environment of local government have increased the necessity to understand group dynamics*
> ♦ *More and more local government officers are finding themselves working in group settings inside and outside the Council.*
> ♦ *Effective group working leads to better work outcomes.*
> ♦ *Managers who understand the content and process elements of group dynamics can enhance their performance in teams and meetings.*

■ INTRODUCTION

The increasing fragmentation within local governments, due in part to external competition and the introduction of internal markets, has increased the importance of understanding the psychology of group behaviour. There exists within different local governments a tension between the tendency of groups who offer similar expertise to compete as opposed to co-operate within the internal market. Equally changes in the external environment mean that local governments are seeking new partnerships with private and other public sector bodies. All these developments require a greater understanding of behaviour in group settings. Achieving effective work outcomes in groups is a skilled process and requires an understanding of group behaviour.

This chapter, will discuss the importance of groups for managers, the factors that influence group cohesiveness, the stages of group development, why work groups get blocked, and effective communication in groups . The purpose is to offer you some insights and frameworks which you can consider in dealing with groups in your working life. It will be useful when thinking about groups to remember the discussion on 'content' and 'process' in Chapter 2.

■ THE IMPORTANCE OF GROUPS TO MANAGERS

It has been clear since the early days of psychological research that people's behaviour is modified when they join a group. It was Gordon Allport that coined the term **social facilitation** to refer to his finding that an improvement occurred in individual performance in the presence of others. At the same time it was noted that a decrease in performance was also possible in the presence of others. Common sense and science can tell us that a decrease in performance in the presence of others is often due to a lack of skill in the activity we are asked to demonstrate or unfamiliarity with those observing us, or a difference in status (higher or lower) in relation to us. Hence the golden rule for presentations: plan them, rehearse them, time them and of course check the equipment. The point is if we are so affected by the mere presence of others, how much more is going on when we are interacting with others in a group.

It has been said that groups are the life-blood of an organisation. They are the building-blocks which are organised to achieve the different organisational tasks. Local government is no different in this regard from other organisations except perhaps in the composition of the groups and the extent of group meetings that are scheduled. As a manager you will have participated in a variety of ways in relation to groups. These will include:

- setting up departmental or inter-departmental groups to achieve tasks and designating someone to lead the group

- participating in departmental or inter-departmental groups as a member

- leading groups (project groups for example)

- reporting and/or being part of departmental groups, chief officers group, to committees

- involvement in working party groups representing the authority's interest in public/private partnership groups and so on.

When we spend time thinking about it we are aware that at any given time in a local authority there are large number of groups each pursuing different goals and composed of different employees. People will join these groups for different reasons: simply because they were nominated, told, were interested, had a vested interest, volunteered, group had high status, it was part of their job, to name but a few. There are a myriad of reasons, but the art of good management is to ensure that irrespective of the reasons for joining the group, performance is effective. While it is absolutely true that people join groups for a variety of reasons, the manager is helped by the fact that two reasons generally dominate groups at work.

1 To accomplish a task. This is becoming increasingly necessary in local government as more and more tasks require an ever-increasing range of specialised skills which are brought together in multi-disciplinary teams. In fact tasks, as against routines, are an increasing feature of the new local government.

2 To satisfy the basic needs of the individual member these needs are as outlined in Maslow's hierarchy of needs i.e. physical, security, social, status recognition and inner achievement of purpose.

The manager is seeking to have groups that could be described as follows: A collection of individuals who share a common set of **norms** and who generally have differentiated roles, and who interact with one another to jointly pursue **common goals**.

■ FACTORS YOU NEED TO CONSIDER WHEN SEEKING EFFECTIVE GROUP PERFORMANCE

Task group individual

The mere existence of a group does not ensure that it will operate effectively; a group is effective only to the degree to which it is able to use its individual and collective resources. The measure of the group's effectiveness in organisational behavioural terms is its ability to achieve its objectives (**task**) and satisfy the needs of the **individuals** within the group. Sometimes the two functions are compatible with one another; on other occasions they may be incompatible, so that a conflict of interest and priorities for the individual and group occur. Consider a departmental management team working as a group to reorganise the departmental structure. As an individual each member has a patch to protect, as a departmental team they have the task to restructure, to reflect the demands of the new environment. How such a task is structured by the Chief Officer will be all-important.

One successful approach I directly observed in a Planning Department in a Metropolitan Borough Council was, to focus the management group, and through them the whole department, on how to organise themselves to deliver a more integrated service to the people they served. Keeping the focus on the needs of internal and external customers meant that individuals had to focus outwards from their own position. The second strategy was not to engage in devising any organisational charts to explain the ideas. The whole focus was, 'how do we achieve an
Cont'd

integrated service for customers'. This Chief Officer understood very well the professional and territorial tendencies of his colleagues, and the need for him as manager to encourage exploration of new ways of tackling the external demands while supporting the departmental management team to remain an effective work group. This process style approach to restructuring did lead the department to reorganise on the basis of delivering an integrated service to the public which meant that internal departmental barriers had to go.

John Adair (1986) is the person most associated with the model that our chief planning officer was working to. It is indeed the model used by the Fire Service to train fire officers in successful leadership roles. The model is depicted as having three overlapping circles named task, group and individual (see Figure 3.1).

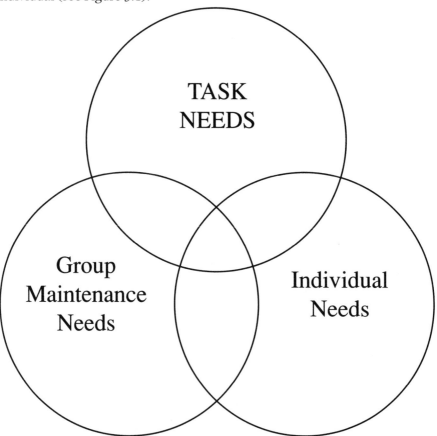

Figure 3.1: Interaction of needs within the group.
Source: Adair J. *Action Centred Leadership*, Gower Press (1979) p. 10.

Task

The model is based on the concept of needs, needs of the task, needs of the group, needs of the individual. In essence Adair is suggesting that groups take on a personality of their own, this of course, being different from group to group. Contingency theory would say it was dependent on situational and task factors. The prime issue that the manager must remember about the task of a group is that the group will be more likely to stay together if they can accomplish the task. We can all recall the working party which just fades away over time due to lack of achievement or the project group working on some agenda which is no longer a priority. When the task loses its centrality the effect on the group is great. After all, this is why they are together, what they focus on, what they need to achieve. The task is usually seen in terms of activities and things rather than people.

Group

The group has a need to develop good working relationships so that the task can be achieved. Adair calls this maintenance needs. Here he is highlighting the need for individual members of the group to work in a manner that is productive for the group. People must listen to one another, consider each other's ideas, build on them for task solutions.

Individual

No person is an island. Each brings to the group a number of individual needs which they may believe working in the group can satisfy. This makes us aware of the important fact that people work to satisfy different needs. Maslow has described these needs as being strictly hierarchical in nature and stated that a need once satisfied it is no longer a motivator. While we can see the flaws in these ideas, the five needs identified by Maslow provide a useful model for understanding why people are motivated to perform work tasks. Maslow reminds us that people work to satisfy basic needs of hunger and thirst. When these are satisfied we work to satisfy our need for safety and security. Again when these are satisfied we work to feel social recognition, friendship, a sense of belonging. Then next we work to satisfy our need for status and finally we work to achieve our full potential as human beings. Of course it is true that what motivates individuals is dependent on their particular circumstances in time and place. Nevertheless in local government today with such a high degree of uncertainty and change in relation to Local Government Review we can immediately see that all five of these needs are relevant to us.

As a manager you will be seeking to acquire a balance between the three overlapping circles. It is of course perfectly appropriate that the working group concentrate at some stages very heavily on the task requirements.

Remember in Chapter 2 I spoke about **content**. You can think of **task** in the same way. The **process** element from Chapter 2 can be directly associated with the idea of the **group** and how it conducts its business. It is very important for time to be spent on the group processes so that the group maintains the momentum for action and of course individuals need to feel the outcome is achieving something for them. When these elements combine well together we say the group is cohesive.

Group roles/functions

It is very difficult to separate management from how the group performs. So much depends on how the group has been set up, the brief they have been given, the degree of authority they feel they have to take action, how much real autonomy they possess from their line department. One needs to ask the question are the results achieved by this group going to be acted upon? The negative side of organisational behaviour can mean that officers are asked by other officers to participate in group tasks which are never going to be implemented. How individual managers become aware of such situations and handle them will depend on their ability to read organisational politics, (*see* Chapter 2). These are all factors which will influence the organisational behaviour of the group. In practical terms, however, certain functions/roles must be undertaken in the group if the group is to achieve the task. The manager can seek to influence the behaviour of the group by having these roles in her/his mind. I find it useful to consider these roles around the three overlapping circles of **Task, Group, Individual**. The roles I am going to describe are a composite view based on extensive research on working groups and leadership undertaken in America in the 1940s and 1950s by people like Bales. In the UK, Trist and Bamworth, and Belbin were looking at these issues in the 1950s and 60s. Many others in the 1970s and 1980s, like Hackman and Fiedler in America, have added to these initial findings. What is most interesting is that those early findings still hold good today.

Task related roles Here we are considering those functions which will initiate action and decisions focused on achieving the task. We may divide them into the following roles:

Solution finders offer new ideas about how to tackle the problem as well as making suggestions about how to solve group difficulties which may relate to how the group is organised or the methods of working.

Information exchangers seek to clarify the exact detail and conditions surrounding the task; they may go outside the group to acquire more information relevant to the task.

Expert advisers speak from knowledge and experience of the issue being tackled. They offer knowledge that is pertinent to the problem.

Synthesisers find the interconnections between different ideas and suggestions, and try to co-ordinate the activities of the group members into working on a solution.

Monitors evaluate what the group is suggesting; they are concerned with the logic and practicality of what is being put forward, and they may have alternate suggestion/solution.

Group relation roles These are concerned with the process issues of the group and are as follows:

Supporters encourage others by being positive about ideas generated in the group; they are warm and enthusiastic about the group activity. They give positive feedback to group members.

Facilitators are conscious of the group as a whole. They seek to encourage contributions from all members, to reduce tension in the group and to manage any conflict positively through constructive group discussion.

Completers are concerned with the quality of what the group is producing and with the group's ability to keep to its schedule. They often give a detailed plan of what is required to achieve the discussed solution.

Workers are prepared to undertake tasks on which the group decides, and are co-operative members of the group while not necessarily wishing to involve themselves in generating solutions.

Individually focused roles These are primarily concentrated on individual members' own needs which may not be relevant or productive for the group. We can observe the following roles:

Blockers are excellent at finding reasons why the task cannot be achieved, is irrelevant, will not work in the department concerned. One strategy they use is to raise an issue that has already been well discussed and rejected by the group and seek to recommence the way forward from there.

Status seekers are very conscious of hierarchy, and of course local government is structured to encourage such a tendency. They may wish to listen only to those of equal or higher rank than themselves. Often they find it difficult to come to terms with ideas and solutions generated by members with special knowledge but lower rank.

Pole position seekers move to manipulate the group so that they can be in a dominating position. They can choose interesting strategies of flattery or exclusion in seeking to attract attention to their position. We can observe them interrupting some members of the group or talking to someone while another member is still putting forward a suggestion. Sometimes they align themselves strongly with a sub-group and seek to encourage that group to dominate the others.

Non-participants adopt a system of non-engagement with the action. They often manifest very passive behaviour which they perceive will insulate them from involvement in the task.

From the above descriptions it is obvious as a manager you will be seeking to form a group that is weighted towards the task and group roles. Equally as a member of a group you would be seeking to move the group towards the activities associated with those areas. Research shows that individuals are capable of playing a variety of roles within a group just as they do in real life. This framework can help you explore the dynamics of your work groups as manager and participant.

At the same time we have to recognise the realities of our own and others' organisational behaviour. What other factors might be helpful to us in managing groups? These are often discussed under the broad term group structure and organisational behaviour.

■ GROUP STRUCTURE AND ORGANISATIONAL BEHAVIOUR

Here I want to consider the following factors: group size, group norms, and group power relationships.

Group size From research we know that the optimal size for an effective group is between six and eight members. As a group increases in size problems arise in terms of communication and co-ordination, not to mention ensuring implementation. Since from research and experience I have found this to be true, I am often quietly amused at the size of Chief Officers' Management Teams in local government. While it is difficult to state categorically when a group loses cohesiveness it is generally thought to be when the group exceeds ten members. Beyond this size the group tends to divide into sub-groups. Of course this happens in local government usually on the basis of status or vested interest and the sub-groups that emerge are often informal and powerful.

Group Norms are the rules and behaviour patterns which are accepted and expected by the group members. We may find ourselves joining groups where the norms are already well established. Hackman (1976) reviewed the available research on group norms in work settings and put forward five important characteristics of group norms.

1 Norms are structural characteristics of groups.

2 Norms only apply to behaviour, private acceptance is not necessary, only public compliance.

3 Norms are generally only developed for important behaviour as defined by the group.

4 Norms develop gradually during the life of the group.

5 All norms do not apply to all members. They can be based on seniority, sex, race and economic class.

In behavioural terms you can seek to establish norms of behaviour in a group which will counteract the non-constructive behaviours of some members of the group. For example in a multi-status group you might seek to establish from the beginning that while in the group all individual contributions would receive equal hearing. It is important to remember that once norms are established and accepted then individual breaches of those norms must either have clear sanctions attached to them or the norms themselves must be questioned and re-evaluated. Equally compliance with the norms must have clear rewards such as recognition and acceptance within the group. Both rewards and sanctions are important because in general the norms of the group define the kind of behaviour the group believes will be conducive to the group achieving the task.

Group power relations Here we are concerned with social power. Within groups it is often observable in behavioural terms that people exercise different forms of social power to reinforce roles and norms. French and Raven (1968) have identified five main sources of power which people use to influence the behaviour of others. These are:

Reward power. This is based on a perception that the person doing the influencing can reward you for compliance in some way. This may range from vague approval to increased responsibilities, to direct promotion, to pay awards.

Punishment power. Here the person who is being influenced believes that non-compliance will have negative effects. This may range from social exclusion to allocation of boring work, to elimination from promotional prospects.

Referent power. Here the person wishes to identify with the influencer because the person is admired, respected, seen as charismatic.

Expert power. Here the influencer relies on superior knowledge or reputation of an expert role to gain the others' agreement to suggestions. This is closely associated with the idea of credibility. For example if the task to be achieved had a strong financial basis accountants could use referent power.

Legitimate power. This is based on the belief of others in the group that the person seeking to influence them has a legitimate right to do so. This often comes from positional power in the hierarchy or from power designated within the group to a leader.

Research by Kipnis *et al.* (1980) showed that in work settings people are resistant to influence attempts. In particular subordinates dislike the use of reward and punishment power. However, when individuals perceive the influence attempts to be either referent, expert or legitimate they are less likely to resist. Local government has a high regard for professional expertise and takes account of positional power and no doubt like all people local government officers are susceptible to referent power.

So in seeking effective group performance a manager needs to consider size, norms and power relations as well as task, group and individual. The question surely arises, are there any stages that one can observe from a behavioural point of view which would assist in deciding whether the group are working effectively or not? This is where Tuckman's (1965) model of group development is a very useful tool. I have used this extensively with local government groups and together we found it helpful for exploring group processes. Tuckman identified four stages in a groups development; these are Forming, Storming, Norming and Performing. I would like to add another for consideration, that is, Ceasing.

Stage 1 Forming

At this stage the group comes together for the first time. There is often a high degree of uncertainty, people may be feeling anxious, or confident they have the situation in hand. Either way the behaviours that manifest themselves often include being quiet, reserved, noisy, and pompous. In reality people are weighing one another up. Individuals are wondering how they stand in relation to this or that person or to the group as a whole. A prime concern at this stage is not to make a fool of oneself. Many groups contain members who know something about each other already. This can mean that risk-taking is very low. Preliminary discussion of the task takes place; the terms of reference and the structures. We can observe during this stage individual attempts to create an impression or establish one's identity. Can you think back to a new group you joined and what you said when asked to introduce yourself? Here is a cameo of an introduction to a new group unfamiliar with one another:

I am Jayne Smith, Deputy Treasurer responsible for a budget of 400 million, I have direct responsibility for 160 staff, I report directly to the Treasurer and am on several interdepartmental project groups taking an authority focus. I am secretary of my regional professional body.

Behind these factual lines lies a claim to expert knowledge and position power. We all indulge in this behaviour to varying degrees when we join such a group for the first time.

Stage 2 Storming

At this stage relationships begin to develop. Group members have begun to discuss the task and are beginning to vie for positions of power and influence. The group can display a wide range of ideas, as people make contributions aimed at both task achievement and moves towards personal influence. In a sense members are jockeying for position. Disagreements will be expressed and ideas will be challenged. The tentative position arrived at in Stage 1 may be challenged, and this can give rise to conflict and hostility. This stage of storming can be very productive because the group, if successful, will move quickly towards operational arrangements for the task.

Stage 3 Norming

Now the group is concerned to create an environment which is conducive to achieving the task. They will begin to prepare time frames, agree standards of performance, develop norms of acceptable behaviour. The group has begun to be comfortable with one another and develop a sense of shared understandings.

Stage 4 Performing

At this stage group members have formed a strong group identity. Often such groups are characterised by a degree of informality, humour and a high level of support for one another. The group focuses on achieving the task and individuals receive a high degree of satisfaction from both the content of what they are undertaking and the behavioural processes used to achieve it. There is a danger for such a cohesive group that they might be reluctant to have a newcomer join them at this stage. Equally they can become insular in their approach and not take enough account of the external environment.

Stage 5 Ceasing

Many groups are established with a set time framework for the task. On completion of the task the group disbands. Equally many groups are formed without time parameters. There is in the life of most groups a stage when the option of ceasing should be considered. We can often note this ourselves as members of a group when we find it very difficult to introduce any new or creative ideas to the group. This is often a sign that apathy is approaching. The skill is to recognise the signs and disband while members still have positive feelings about the group experience.

The usefulness of this model lies in the fact that you can observe groups getting blocked at these stages of development. Not every group becomes a high performing group, often because of a combination of the factors discussed above. If you are managing groups, or part of a group, with thoughtful observation you may be able to help them overcome the blocks and become performing groups in Tuckman's terminology.

As the penultimate point I wish to discuss the role of leadership in group behaviour, followed by some thoughts on how groups can contribute to corporate strategic management within authorities.

Group leadership

There have been extensive studies of how the leadership role can emerge in a group. One of the main findings is that leaders can adopt two approaches. One is to become a task leader. The task leader offers a correct solution to the group. While she or he can demonstrate a way of achieving the task they are likely to remain in a leadership role. The other option is to become a leader by concentrating on the social emotional needs of the group. This of course fits neatly with Adair's model of group needs. Interestingly research also shows that it is quite difficult to find in one person the ability to be both a task leader and a social emotional leader. I think local government would reflect that experience as well. We have tended to concentrate on developing content expertise or professionalism. Officers are primarily promoted on the basis of expert knowledge and then expected to manage people.

Fiedler reminds us of a very important factor that affects group leadership. In essence he suggests that leadership behaviour is dependent on the favourability of the leadership situation. He highlights three important variables that influence the situation:

Leader-member relations This refers to the amount of trust and liking the members are willing to give the leader

The task structure This is related to the degree of clarity with which the task has been defined for the group and how easy it is to carry out the task as a routine set of procedures.

Position Power The actual position of the leader in the organisation, what is her/his level in the hierarchy. What rewards and sanctions can the leader impose, whom can the leader influence.

One of the most important things that Fiedler's work points out is that leadership in groups, as elsewhere, is a two way process. Where there are leaders there are followers. Secondly, leadership is often dependent on the situation; you may believe you are a natural leader/manager but is that just because of your position in the organisation? What happens in your own peer group, do you emerge as leader there?

■ THE USE OF GROUPS IN CORPORATE STRATEGIES

An enduring characteristic of local government is the tension between departmentalism and corporatism. This problem is often portrayed as service departments wishing to be masters of their own destiny and resenting policy inputs or charges for support services from central or support departments. It is equally true that central and service departments find difficulties in working together, to provide one service to a particular client group. When we think about this strategically we see the need to find ways where we can celebrate the validity of working separately and working in association with one another. In reality local government has known this to be an issue for some time. However current practices within local authorities make it difficult to counteract the negative aspects of either excessive departmentalism or corporatism. Here I refer to the way we generally use interdepartmental groups on corporate issues. The procedure is normally to nominate a departmental representative to work on the issue. The working group will then submit a report to be considered by the initiating agent. In organisational terms group members feel they are there to represent the interests of their departments. This motivation can be stronger than the desire to find the best corporate solution. There is often concern because nominated members are unclear as to the degree of authority they have to act on behalf of their department. This leads to an increase in meetings, because members wish to check with their departments before resolution. Alternatively this does not happen, and the meeting just drifts on. The most significant fault with this procedure is that it separates the policy initiators from those who are considering how to operationalise it. This leaves the gate open for the initiators of the working group to reject the suggested solution or to adopt it, but implementation demonstrates no real ownership of the solution.

One way of resolving this kind of unsatisfactory outcome is to use groups more strategically, by ensuring that you close the gap between those who initiate working groups and those who undertake the work within them. This would require a much more process-oriented approach to group working based on three key factors: **trust, delegated authority** and **ownership**. Here is the basis of the approach. By trust I mean the common agreement within the authority that when officers are working separately on issues they are doing so on behalf of the whole. Delegated authority refers to the need for members of working groups to be clear about the extent of authority they have in their role as a group member. This is a move away from what I call a permission culture that often exists between differential hierarchies within departments. Ownership is concerned with closing the gap between the initiators of the working group, the working members and their work outcomes. The key here is not to permit working groups to submit reports to initiators in the normal, rather sterile way of written reports to management teams.

An alternative approach on the basis of the above three factors would be for a small working group or several small groups to work on an issue. Well before resolution the group/s should convene with the initiator/s and other stakeholders to gauge reactions to the proposed direction The format for this exchange should be like a brain-storming feedback session. Flip charts and pens for a very relaxed approach. This kind of session might occur more than once in the generation of a solution. This process style approach can tackle the issue of ownership, commitment and communication. If your Chief Officer Manager will not come to such an event, having nominated you for the working group, how committed is he/she to its resolution? The process is aimed at gathering in an open forum the views and commitment of important stakeholders. It does require a fundamental shift, but it is based on sound evidence as to how groups work best and does address in a process way the issue of departmentalism and corporatism.

■ IMPLICATIONS FOR YOU, THE MANAGER

To analyse a group at work is a complex and difficult task. It means not only observing the group and its members but also being aware of how your own behaviour impacts on others and contributes to the character of the group. Below is a list of questions that could be used to explore the dynamics of group behaviour. This list is by no means exhaustive and can be used in a variety of ways. The intention is just to jog your memory about the issues raised in this chapter:

1 Is the group more focused on task, group or the individual?
2 What roles are the individual members of the group undertaking? Are these roles contributing to group performance?
3 Who has been more task-oriented?
   Who has been more concerned for the social and emotional needs of

the group?

4 Has one person emerged as group leader? Or has the leader varied according to task and circumstances?

5 Do some members contribute more to discussion than others?

6 Are some members shy and retiring, and how is that dealt with in the group?

7 Have any sub-groups developed within the group?

8 What kind of influence attempts are being used by members of the group?

9 At what stage of development do you think the group has arrived?

10 What norms has the group established?

11 Does the size of the group affect performance?

12 Have members of the group learnt from one another?

13 How would you describe the atmosphere in the group, formal or informal?

14 Is the group prepared to listen to the external environment?

References

Adair, J. (1986) *Effective Teambuilding*. Gower Publishing Co Ltd, Aldershot

Bales, R.F. (1950) 'A Set of categories for the Analysis of Small Group Interaction', *American Sociological Review* (Vol.15, April, pp.257–63)

Belbin, M. (1981) *Management Teams: Why They Succeed or Fail*. Heinemann, London

Fiedler, F.E. and Mahar, L. (1979) 'The Effectiveness of Contingency Model Training: A Review of the Validation of Leader Match'. *Personnel Psychology*, (32, pp.45–62)

Hackman, J.R. (1976) 'Group Influences in Individuals' in Dunnette, M. D. (ed.) *Handbook of Industrial and Organisational Psychology*. Rand McNally, Chicago

French, J. and Raven B.(1968) 'The Bases of Social Power', in Cartwright, D. and Zander, A.F. (eds), *Group Dynamics Research and Theory*. 3rd Edn. Harper and Row, New York

Kipnis, D., Schmidt, S.M. and Wilkinson, I. (1980) 'Intra-organisational Influence Tactics: Explorations in getting one's way', *Journal of Applied Psychology* (Vol.65, 4, pp.440–452)

Maslow, A. H. (1970) *Motivation and Personality*. Harper and Row, New

York

Tuckman, B. W. (1965) 'Development Sequence in Small Groups', *Psychological Bulletin* (Vol.63, pp.384–99).

Trist, E.I. and Bamworth, W. (1951) 'Some social and psychological consequences of the long-wall method of coal getting', *Human Relations* (4)

4

Recruitment and selection

Key points

◆ The trend towards a decentralised personnel function increases the need for individual manager to think carefully about recruitment and selection.

◆ Effective requirement and selection mean that the manager acquires a staff member who can make an effective contribution immediately.

◆ For the manager to achieve effective recruitment and selection requires knowledge of job analysis, recruitment procedures, selection techniques and the barriers to effective selection.

■ INTRODUCTION

The continuously changing environment in which local government officers undertake their roles and the ever increasing demand for effective performance make the role of recruitment and selection central to the management of human resources. The competitive nature of a major proportion of the work undertaken by local authorities means that new recruits at whatever level are required to be able to perform effectively almost immediately. This is particularly true of posts linked to short-term contracts. The fact that in many authorities the personnel function has been decentralised to departments means that recruitment and selection is undertaken by departments within policy frameworks and guidelines. This requires managers to know, understand and use recruitment and selection effectively. This chapter takes an individualistic view. It looks at recruitment and selection from the perspective of the manager seeking to fill a post.

■ QUESTIONS YOU NEED TO ASK WHEN A VACANCY OCCURS

When a vacancy does present itself there are several questions that must be addressed:

Do you need to refill that post? This may be the opportunity to redesign posts in a particular section so that jobs may be enriched or enlarged, giving more responsibility and recognition to staff. On the other hand the decision not to fill the post may be influenced by a need to make savings. Such a decision needs to be balanced against the effects on the motivation of staff when posts are not filled. I have heard many officers say 'we could do so much better if we had our full establishment figure'. This is one of those statements that are difficult to prove or disprove.

Where does this job fit into the overall human resource plan? The filling of the post should not be in isolation in the sense of finding someone who can just do this job. It may be necessary to look at the potential of candidates for training, management development and future promotional potential. In addition, with the pace of change in local government it may be necessary to assess candidates adaptability and flexibility to changing working conditions. For example could this person work from home and still produce the outcomes in terms of time and quality?

What personal competences as against technical competencies does the job holder require to perform the job effectively? There is no point in appointing someone who is technically superb and then discovering that he/she is not able to undertake the networking and influencing aspects of the post, for example.

Should the job be filled internally or should the job be open to external and internal competition? The answer here is related to two main considerations. Firstly what do your equal opportunities policies state in this regard for this particular post? Secondly, you must consider the motivational aspects of staff internal to the organisation wishing to see opportunities for movement within the authority, against the value of perhaps selecting some external candidate who will bring an outside perspective to bear on issues. There is the long-established rationale in local government for including external candidates as a means of testing internal candidates against the marketplace to see if the internal is really worthy. My question here is, should you not know that already? Within the policy of equal opportunities I would not recommend external candidates unless you really mean to appoint one, if they prove the best on the day.

What do I need to consider to comply with the personnel and equal opportunities policies of the Authority in relation to this post? While all authorities comply with the legal requirements the strength of these policies differs across authorities. So here it is useful to remember a simple guiding principle. Your role is to ensure that all people who could do the job effectively have equal opportunity to apply and that all who apply are treated with justice and fairness. If you are uncertain as to how to guarantee this, then you will need to seek the advice of your central/core personnel department.

Having considered these questions your ideas are now taking shape; this is the time to ensure that the following activities occur. You may, or may not carry them out yourself.

■ THE VALUE OF A GOOD JOB ANALYSIS

Job analysis consists of the systematic and logical examination of a job in sufficient detail to identify: component tasks, skills and knowledge requirements, other job content information, demands on the job holder and other modified factors relative to the specific purpose of the analysis. Its importance lies in the fact that from the job analysis are derived a job description and a job specification. The job description and job specification will together influence the content of the advertisement and hence the sample of candidates who apply for the post. Here are two working definitions of a job description and job specification.

Job description: A job description tells you about the broad purpose, total requirements, component tasks, duties and responsibilities of the job; and where this job stands in relation to other posts within the organisation. The quantity and detail of information vary according to the purpose for which it is used and the personnel practices of the authority.

Job specification: This should be seen as an extension of the job description because it not only tells you about the job, but importantly makes a detailed statement on the 'ideal candidate'. This will include qualifications and experience, intellectual abilities, personal skills, physical characteristics, special requirements (for example clean driving licence). In compiling a job specification special attention must be paid to equal opportunity policies.

Local government has a long history of job descriptions being available for all posts (varying in quality and amount of detail), and a shorter history of job specifications.

The following is an example of the headings on a Standard Job Description: Job Title, Department, Section, Grade, Function, Qualifications. Responsible to: Other relationships, Duties/Activities, Conditions.

The following example is of a Job Description Control Sheet which is used to provide immediate knowledge on how current the information is on a particular job. The job description control sheet is attached to the Job Description.

Job Description Control Sheet

Department,	*Division,*	*Section*
Job Designation	*Grade*	
Post No.	*No. of Posts*	
Responsible to:	*Responsible for*	Directly, Indirectly,
Car Allowance		
Special Conditions		

Is Job Analysis Available?   Yes/No

Education Requirements
Basic

Professional

Experience/Knowledge/Skills Required
Essential

Revision of Job Description

Date   Nature of Change

Job Description

Post Objectives

Key areas   *Key Tasks*

While this example may still be the closest to the dominant trend in local government, there are an increasing number of job descriptions written in terms of key result areas, reflecting the emphasis on effective performance. When key result areas are used to describe the job, the emphasis is on the quality of the outcomes required from the job holder. This then requires translation into guidance on selection.

The real concern of the manager is to have as accurate a picture as possible of what the job requires, in terms of knowledge and skills and the personal abilities needed for effective performance. You acquire this information from a job analysis. Briefly job analysis covers five main areas, two of which we have discussed (Job Description, Job Specification). The others are Job Comparison, Criterion Development, Improvement Factors.

Job comparison: Here information is required so that a comparison can be made with other jobs inside or outside the organisation. The obvious example is job evaluation; this assists in recruitment decisions about grade and pay to be offered for the job. It also very useful to the manager in undertaking elements of career planning, or job secondments.

Criterion Development: Here information is required to assist in the development of criteria for assessing performance, an obvious example being performance appraisal systems as well as those for recruitment and selection procedures. For example you may want to know how a particularly difficult situation was dealt with, and use this as an in-tray exercise for the selection process.

Improvement Factors: Here the intention is to identify aspects of organisational activities that interact with the job, that can be improved. Examples would be personal competence, working conditions, the work activities, the linkages between this job and others in the organisation. Identification of improvement factors can contribute to a more tightly defined job in terms of tasks and skill requirements.

These are five areas that the job analysis seeks to address. The next question is, whom should you involve in the information-gathering process? The following should definitely be included:

Job incumbent: The manager needs to consider that the job holder has the most detailed information on the job requirements. This must be taken account of. The information must be looked at for bias and or omission. Sometimes we know something so well that we just do not mention it as significant.

Line Manager: The manager will be aware that the line manager will have his/her own view of what the job entails and what the organisation expects. However the line manager is unlikely to be fully aware of what the job entails, even if he/she previously held such a post. We know that jobs change over time.

Other members of the 'role set': The manager may consider that subordinates, peers and others with whom the job holder interacts, e.g. customers/clients, may be a useful source of information for analysis.

Your authority may have technical experts who specialise in this area. Then all you need to ensure is that they consult with the people as outlined above. If such technical experts are not available, your prime purpose is to achieve a job description and job specification, which tells you the **critical requirements in terms of qualifications, experience, skills, knowledge and personal attributes needed by candidates to perform the job effectively**. Without this you are severely at a disadvantage going into the recruitment and selection process.

One of the standard aids to this process much used in the UK is Rodger's Seven Point Plan. The concept is that before going to the recruitment and selection stage you know the profile required for the job in the following areas according to Rodger's Seven Point Plan:

1 physical make-up (health, physique, appearance, bearing, speech)
2 attainments (education, training, experience, degree of success in each)
3 general intelligence
4 special aptitudes (mechanical, numerical, verbal, drawing, music, manual dexterity)
5 interests (intellectual, practical, social, artistic, physically active)
6 disposition (dependability, self-reliance)
7 circumstances (domestic, family, special)

These seven areas are then used to construct a series of questions that relate to the candidate and which must be interpreted in light of the demands of the job.

Recruitment checklist

As a manager you know the need to attract suitable applicants for the job. This is a huge area which I intend to concentrate on only briefly because most local authorities have well worked out systems for recruitment that actively seek to ensure that all eligible candidates will have an opportunity to apply. I offer you a check list of items as an aid to memory:

1 Internal/external advertisement
2 Use of recruitment agencies
3 Where to place the job advertisement (national, local, specialist press)
4 The cost of the advertisement, its content, its presentation and a system to monitor responses
5 The quality and appropriateness of the application form for the particular post
6 An information pack for candidates
7 How the job offer is going to be made to the successful candidate
8 How to reimburse the expenses of candidates who participate in the selection process

Having decided on and completed the recruitment procedures which in essence leave you with a clear list of the **critical requirements for the job**, you are now faced with deciding what selection methods you should use, to help you select the best candidate for the job.

■ THE BEHAVIOURAL ASPECTS OF THE DIFFERENT SELECTION TECHNIQUES

The methods of selection involve the screening of the application forms against the list of critical requirements for the job, the assessment of information about the applicants, often in the form of references, and the design and preparation of the selection process. There exists a wide choice of selection techniques for the manager intending to design a selection process. One could be very positive and say that this is a good thing, but this has to be tempered by the fact that selection is a very difficult area. The wide choice reflects the need to use several techniques in one selection process in an effort to counterbalance the inherent weaknesses of the various instruments.

The manager engaged in the selection process has formed a view as to the kind of employee behaviour required for the job. It may be that the job requires skills in working in groups or teams. From then on the manager is seeking to make a judgement about their future job performance based on the behaviour of the candidates in the selection process. In this sense the manager is trying to predict future outcomes. Logically we all know the fallibility of trying to foretell the future, but we often forget that this is what we are seeking to do in selection. The whole issue of whether selection is an art or a science is linked to the question of prediction. The manager may take the view that it is possible to have unambiguous selection criteria which, once measured and statistically analysed, clearly predict candidates' future performance. If this is the case, then selection could clearly be a science. On the other hand, the manager may believe that making an assessment of human potential is so complex , that no measurement tool combined with statistical analysis could ever produce a strong enough prediction ratio. In this case the manager is coming to the selection process with a belief in selection as an art. This is a huge debate, well beyond the scope of this chapter. I draw your attention to it because the general view underlying selection in local government is that one should move as closely as possible to the scientific end of the continuum. This is required to fulfil equal opportunity aspects of selection, in particular the necessity for objectivity, consistency and validity in the process of selection. Two words are key here, **reliability** and **validity**.

Reliability: In the context of selection the manager must ensure that candidates for a particular job are assessed in the same way. The purpose is to build into the process consistency and objectivity. For example if you are interviewing several candidates you should ask each candidate the same interview questions in the same order. This allows you to compare answers from all candidates at the end of the interviewing process.

Validity: In the context of selection the manager must ensure that any selection method used is capable of testing relevant job requirements. There would be little point in testing a candidate's mechanical aptitude if the test assesses only the ability to do the test and does not indicate how well candidates will be able to do a mechanical related job. We often say people are good interviewees. What we mean is that the interview has low validity because it does not predict very well the future job performance of candidates. Candidates can pass the test but it is not related to subsequent job performance.

As a manager, once you have considered the implications of ensuring reliability and validity in the selection process, you are most likely to be concerned with considering the face-to-face techniques for selecting applicants for employment. Here you are concerned with two areas. One is discovering whether the candidates can actually do the job as advertised, and the second, whether the candidates have the ability to perform tasks that may or may not be specified as yet. You may like to think of the latter as the candidates' potential for future performance.

Choosing selection methods

The interview is the most used method in the selection process. There is overwhelming evidence to suggest that it is a very fallible instrument. However both interviewers and interviewees like it very much, so its use is likely to continue as the most popular selection tool from a behavioural point of view. As a manager your concern will be how to balance the certainty of using some form of interview in the selection process with other selection methods that permit the candidates to display their abilities and potentialities. The decision as to what selection methods to use must be linked to the level of the post and the list of critical criteria that have emerged from the job analysis. There is evidence from Smith (1988) that ability tests, biodata and personality questionnaires reach an acceptable level of predictability with the validity coefficient of 0.30 being the lowest acceptable criterion. Other studies show that interviews reach only a validity coefficient of 0.14. Given the extensive use of the interview and its low validity, I wish to concentrate on its use as a tool in selection from a behavioural perspective. First, however, I want to discuss briefly some other selection methods under the headings of Ability, Biodata, Psychometric Tests and Assessment Centres.

Ability tests

The manager wishing to test the ability/abilities of candidates may choose from a variety of methods depending on the ability or abilities being tested. These include: Group Problem Solving, In Tray Exercises, Presentation Skills, Work Simulation Exercises. All these methods have one thing in common: they seek to permit the candidates to display their abilities in relation to particular work-related criteria. It is essential that the manager has a clear view of what abilities are being assessed and how a comparative judgement is going to be made of all the candidates. This requires a list of the indicators of the ability being tested, and the different weight accorded to each of these indicators of ability.

When internal and external candidates are competing for a post, special attention must be paid as to whether a Work Simulation Exercise is fair. As a manager you would need to ensure that your internal candidates had no extra knowledge of the situation in the work simulation. This is often difficult to guarantee. You might then make a judgement to use a case study problem-solving approach. The content of the case study would focus on an ability you really wished to test. For example financial ability is often an area a manager would seek to test.

Biodata

The application form is usually the major source of biographical data. As a manager it is useful for you to spend some time thinking about the relevance of the application form to the specific job for which the candidate is applying. The candidate spends a considerable amount of time thinking about what to say on the application form. If the questions are really relevant to the job, the form can be a great source of information. In these days of computer technology it should not be a major issue to redesign or modify a form to increase its relevance for particular posts. In the majority of cases candidates answer them truthfully; nevertheless it is wiser to cross-check information about qualifications and experience.

While it is very difficult to make a definitive statement about the perfect application form here are some suggestions for amendments to standard local government forms.

1 A form must ensure that a candidate is contactable. Allowing space for one address is insufficient.

2 A form must ensure that candidates can express the full range of their educational achievements. This means allowing more space for qualifications other than GCSEs, A levels and degrees.

3 A form should state clearly what kind of work experience you wish the candidate to tell you about. You may also wish the candidate to mention work skills and experience which they have, but are currently not using.

4 Ethnic monitoring—this is recommended under the Code of Practice of the Commission for Racial Equality.

5 The form should indicate clearly where to return the application form and when the candidate can expect a reply.

Well designed forms are of use throughout the whole process. Application forms help in pre-selection screening, contribute as pointers for further questioning in the interview process and are of use for comparison against references in relation to a candidate's job achievements. It is worth a manager's time looking at their design.

Psychometric tests

A manager wishing to use psychometric tests should view them as one tool to be used in conjunction with others in the selection process. It is absolutely essential that specialist knowledge is used in the selection and administering of all psychometric tests. The right of individual candidates to feedback about the results of the test must always be guaranteed. Qualified test administrators will have signed a code of practice guaranteeing professional standards. As manager you will need to be reassured that the test once chosen measures what it is supposed to measure, and that the candidate's results can be measured against a representative peer group sample. Tests are of course subject to cultural bias and this must be taken account of.

The concept of using psychometric tests can generate a high degree of hostility or at the very least anxiety. If we take intelligence tests as an example a considerable amount of people believe it inappropriate to be asked to undertake such a test. Another concern is that it takes a high degree of knowledge to choose an appropriate test for a specific job. This is because psychologists themselves disagree about the concept of intelligence, and this has direct implications for the structure and content of various tests. The aim of an intelligence test is to differentiate between different types of mental ability. The complication is that some tests tap a clear-cut dichotomy between verbal ability and numerical ability. On the other hand, others seek to differentiate across such headings as: verbal comprehension, word fluency, number aptitude, inductive reasoning, memory, spatial aptitude, perceptual speed. What we can say is that people get different test scores on intelligence tests. What significance you wish to place on this fact as a manager, should be based on an informed view of how relevant this information has been as an indicator of successful performance on other occasions.

Candidates are not over-keen on the idea of an intelligence test, and they very often feel the same about personality tests. The reservations expressed about personality tests are very similar to those expressed about intelligence tests. The main criticisms relate to the fact that theories of personality are many and varied, and there is doubt as to whether personality can be measured. Personality tests broadly fall into two categories those based on the trait approach to personality, and those based on personality inventories. The trait approach considers that a finite number of traits exists and that they can be measured. Measurement is based on a candidate's responses to a wide variety of situational contexts. The Cattell 16PF is a classic example of this approach. Cattell through extensive research believed that a trait is a 'mental structure', an inference made from observed behaviour to account for its regularity and consistency. In this sense Cattell's work can be regarded as a search for the definitive list of source traits which together give the fundamental structures of the total personality. Cattell has isolated some sixteen to twenty-one source traits. The best-known of these are the sixteen which go to form the Sixteen Personality Factor Questionnaire (16PF Test).

The other approach is to construct personality inventories empirically. The method involves giving hundreds of test questions to groups of individuals known to differ on a particular criterion from the norm. Questions which distinguish between the normal group and the criterion group are retained as questions in the inventory. An example of such a test is the Minnesota Multi-Phase Personality Inventory (MMPI) The MMPI, while not perfect is an example of a personality inventory based on criterion keying. It is composed of ten scales which cover most of the various neurotic and pyschotic disorders. Application of the test demonstrates that your sample is either similar or dissimilar to these criterion groups.

There are problems with validity of the results from Personality Inventories. Problems arise in the following areas:

- It is sometimes easy to see within the Inventory what is a socially acceptable answer rather than a truthful answer.

- The inventories tap into a wide number of traits, and you may be only interested in a few.

- Inventories usually are concerned with general personality profile. As a manager you may be concerned only with work traits. The Occupational Personality Profile a derivative of the 16PF has been developed in UK to address this point.

Despite the problems, managers should not rule out the use of personality tests. The main issue for you as the manager is, will this test add to my knowledge about the candidate? If you decide the test will provide more information about particular traits that are important in the job, then it is worth using a test.

Finally the results from any type of psychometric test should be used in conjunction with other information gathered by the various methods used in the total selection process. The joint results should help you to decide which candidate has the best profile for the job.

Assessment centres

Assessment centres use a range of assessment techniques to decide whether candidates are suitable for particular jobs. Assessment centres do not confine their activities to recruitment and selection. They are also used for development needs and promotional decisions. Assessment centres are a new phenomenon in local government. There is a slightly longer history of using assessment centres than the development of them by particular local authorities. When an authority has a very clear strategic approach to human resource development then an assessment centre can play an important role in human resourcing decisions. For example an authority with a clear view of the competences it seeks in staff at different levels, combined with a manager who has a clear critical requirements profile for a post, makes an effective selection process. Assessment centres perform well in such situations. Assessment centres do have the advantage of giving candidates a better feel for the organisation and its values. This affords the individual more time to decide whether they themselves are willing to fit into the organisation.

While assessment centres differ, a manager thinking of using an assessment centre for selection could expect the approach to include the following features:

- The central approach is on behaviour.
- Exercises are used to simulate the core tasks of the job. Performances in these simulations are believed to predict on the job behaviour.
- Candidates are assessed together to make the process more transparent and interactive.
- Several assessors or observers are used to ensure objectivity. All assessors should have been extensively trained. Since this is not always the case, it is worth seeking confirmation of training.
- The approach to measuring performance is multi-dimensional. Therefore candidates will undergo a range of selection activities from interviews to group exercises, to psychometric tests.

While the cost of using an assessment centre may be high so far their reputation for permitting candidates to display a wide range of abilities is good.

The interview

The interview holds a central place in any selection procedure. A study at McGill University in Canada during the 1950s showed that interviewers decided to accept or reject candidates within the first three or four minutes of the interview. They then spent the rest of the time seeking evidence to support their first impression. These studies also showed that interviewers placed more weight on unfavourable evidence than on evidence that was favourable. Prejudice in this sense is a great time-saver as it allows people to form opinions without having to bother with collecting the facts. In discussing the interview process I want to concentrate on the psychological behavioural aspects of the interview process. Interviewing is too often regarded as an easily performed activity which managers are good at. The truth is much more likely to be that managers are good interviewers because they are been trained and have developed their skills with practice.

Personal barriers to effective interviewing

Earlier in this chapter I mentioned that the process of selection was concerned with prediction. The manager is seeking to make an assessment of candidates' likely future performance on the basis of collected evidence. Here, we come up against the most fundamental barrier to selecting the 'right' candidate, our own limited ability to perceive others accurately. Interviewing candidates is ultimately about the interviewer/s forming personal perceptions about candidates abilities and future performance.

Person perception

Two major factors influence our personal perception of others. First, each of us is directly influenced by our own unique set of experiences. We learn by observing various kind of models: these can be represented by rules and laws, schools, religious institutions, work organisations, literature, art, societal norms and by those people whom we consider to be significant, parents, peers, etc. These unique sets of social experiences influence our beliefs and values and form a basis from which we perceive, interpret and judge the world.

Secondly, as individuals we try to discover cause and effect relations in the events around us. In trying to make sense of our world we make attributions about events and people. In relation to people we try to find out what dispositions other people have. Dispositions are qualities or characteristics of the person such as moods, abilities, personality traits and values. To a person's perceived dispositions we attribute particular outcomes. In other words, we see people as having personalities and skills that make them behave in a certain way. By inferring what an individual's internal characteristics are, we believe we can predict their behaviours. Very simply put we may decide that a person has the personality traits of warmth and friendliness. In our culture evidence shows that we will attribute or predict that this person is capable of generous, honest and tactful behaviours. There may be general agreement about this in UK culture, because of shared cultural experiences. On the other hand an individual may make attributions on an idiosyncratic basis. For example few of us would expect an arrogant person to be patient unless we believed it to be true from our own unique experience.

As managers, then, we need to be aware of just how individualistic our judgements can be in the interview process. One way of safeguarding against this is by involving more than one person in the interviewing process. A group interview situation will result in a comparative discussion of individual perceptions.

Managers are only too well aware of the amount of information they are bombarded with in the workplace. Each of you will have your own way of handling this, from straight transference to the waste bin to a highly organised system of distribution across time allocated in trays. As individuals we also try to organise the vast amount of information we receive into bit-size retainable chunks. One way we do this is by stereotyping.

Stereotyping

Stereotyping is the tendency to assign positive and negative attributes to someone solely on the basis of a category in which the person is placed. All stereotypes are inaccurate because they are simplified for easy recall. The problem with their use in perception is, in recalling the simplified general stereotype of the category in which the person is placed, we fail to acknowledge the characteristics that distinguish the person as an individual. Stereotyping limits our ability to make objective decisions in the interview process. In local government today most managers are aware of the more obvious forms of stereotyping in relation to race, gender, disability and more recently age. If we take age as an example, the classic stereotype in relation to the older applicant includes:

- Older applicants are set in their ways
- Older applicants will not want to learn new things
- Older applicants are physically slow
- Older applicants will not take risks
- Older applicants are reliable
- Older applicants have experience, they can do the job immediately

What is interesting is that the negative view nearly always outweighs the positive view in the interview process, unless the interviewer is prepared to assess the individual. This last point about negative information highlights another concern about how we use information to form judgements.

Expectancy effects

Prior information about an event, activity or person can influence our perception. For example, you have been told that one of the candidates is very intelligent and knowledgeable in her profession. This may lead you on the day of the interview to place more weight on her responses than on those of other candidates. In contrast if we have some negative information about a candidate we find it very difficult to judge them on the basis of the evidence they present on the day. Bad news travels fast is a very accurate saying. As individuals we are susceptible to projecting our own feelings onto the behaviour of others.

Projection

In the context of an interview you may discover that one candidate, if appointed, would have to drive forty miles to the office. You cannot imagine anything more unappealing. The candidate does not appear to be bothered by the prospect, but you as interviewer continue to see it as a problem and allow it to affect your perception of this person as a candidate.

I hope the above has demonstrated how the perceptual processes can result in our making errors of judgement or understanding in a number of ways. Fortunately through training and experience managers can learn to perceive and judge others with more accuracy in the interview process. Here are three key objectives for managers involved in the interviewing process:

Before the interview objective: To ensure that the questions drawn up in order to assess the candidates, are in line with the requirements of the job description and job specification.

During the interview objective: To ensure that each applicant is assessed fairly and equally for the job through the interview process.

After the interview objective: To find the candidate who best matches the job specification.

If as a manager you are unsure about how to tackle any one of these objectives in a way that ensures a fair and just process, then you need to consider interview training.

■ IMPLICATIONS FOR YOU AS MANAGER

The manager seeking to ensure more effective recruitment and selection has to take great care about matching people to the requirements of the organisation as well as to the particular requirements of the job. This means being able to specify the competences, attitudes and characteristics required by candidates to perform the job. There is a need to use a wide variety of methods to select candidates who match the requirements. Although the interview is the most ubiquitous selection tool, managers need to be fully aware of the difficulties experienced by individuals when trying to predict performance from observed behaviour or attributed personality traits.

References

Cattell, R.B. (1963) *The Sixteen Personality Factor Questionnaire (16 PF)*. Institute for Personality and Ability Testing, University of Illinois Press, Illinois.

Cattell, R.B. (1965) *The Scientific Analysis of Personality*. Penguin Books, Harmondsworth

Smith, M. (1988) 'Calculating the sterling value of selection', *Guidance and Assessment Review* (4(1))

5

Motivation and job design

Key points

◆ *Within local government there has been a shift away from the more obvious command and control systems, to more delegated accountability and responsibility.*

◆ *Local governments are also experiencing increased work demands in an environment of constrained resources.*

◆ *The reality which emerges from the first two points is that staff will have to do more with less.*

◆ *In such circumstances it is essential that managers consider carefully what motivates people to work and how jobs might be designed to create a productive working environment.*

■ INTRODUCTION

Essentially local authorities in the past, and indeed to a large extent in the present, can be represented as tall hierarchical structures. Within these structures, as noted in Chapter 4, job descriptions of varied depth and detail define the duties and responsibilities of particular posts. How an organisation designs and creates job spaces tells individuals a lot about their potential relationship with the hierarchy. There is a contemporary shift from command and control to responsibility and accountability. Senior managers in local government tend to display a belief that they should have access to more autonomy and responsibility but that it ought to be rationed to those below them in the hierarchy. This chapter explores when this might be true or false and gives examples of various initiatives within local government of increasing the autonomy of individuals within their jobs while maintaining clear accountabilities. Management delegation in local government has been hindered in many cases not by the schemes of delegation, but by the behaviour of individuals.

■ MOTIVATION—WHAT IS IT?

It would be useful to start at the very beginning by saying why you as managers are concerned with motivation. There are hundreds of definitions in textbooks about what is meant by motivation, but it is more useful first to consider the key points that are likely to concern you as local government managers about motivation of staff. These are:

- what drives behaviour?
- what direction does the behaviour take? Is it in support or against the goals of the organisation/department/division/section?
- how to maintain behaviour that is in the desired direction and reduce or eliminate behaviour which is counter-productive?
- how to ensure goal-directed performance?

Immediately we express those concerns we have to make some important clarifications to ourselves which highlight the dilemma of the link between motivation and performance. Essentially **motivation does not equal performance**. We need to think of the following equation:

$$Performance = (ability \times motivation)$$

Ability is the amount of talent a person has for the task. Talent in this sense can include intellectual properties, content and process competencies, physical strength etc. But a person must want to perform the task, so we are back to motivation. In this sense motivation is the energy we display in the goal-directed behaviour. Therefore we say a person was motivated to behave in a certain way to achieve a particular outcome. If this is true then people are motivated to behave to satisfy a need to achieve a desired objective. This explains why it is possible in performance terms to have two officers, both with the same high level of ability (in this case assume ability to mean content knowledge of the task), one of whom displays a high level of motivation, demonstrated in work tasks and reports being completed on time, the other demonstrating very little motivation with work tasks and reports often late. What distinguishes the performance of the two officers is the difference in motivation. You could of course reverse this example. If motivation was the same but ability levels were different you could still have differential performance.

Here we are touching on the crux of the matter. Motivation is an individual phenomenon. All individuals have their own wants and needs which affect their level of motivation. Equally motivation is intentional behaviour, a person does something because they have chosen to do it. So we often say motivation is what causes behaviour and that we need to distinguish between motivation, behaviour and performance. Here is a useful definition of motivation in the workplace:

Motivation is the result of processes internal or external to the individual, that arouse enthusiasm and persistence to pursue a certain course of action.

This definition recognises an important fact that people are motivated by intrinsic factors and extrinsic factors. We can broadly categorise these in the following way:

Intrinsic factors: feelings of accomplishment, interesting and/or challenging work, internal values accord with the work. These are all integral to the task and are administered by the person doing the task

Extrinsic factors pay, promotions, work conditions, compliments, etc. These are all independent of the task performed and are controlled by other people

The manager contemplating the above factors needs to consider both the intrinsic and extrinsic elements of motivation. It is obvious that everyone cannot be promoted to the highest level, in fact some people would not want to be. In seeking effective performance a manager needs to consider the specific need structure of all employees and then find ways in which work can be undertaken so that intrinsic and extrinsic factors can be maximised. Easy to say, difficult to achieve, one reason being that we as people use a wide range of cognitive thought processes to decide what our action should be. These are often situation-specific. In the last ten years we have seen enormous changes in the context in which work is undertaken in local government. We have observed changes in the organisational behaviour of our colleagues and staff. One clear distinction in the early days of change was between those who have welcomed the introduction of the so-called business culture to local government and others who found this inappropriate and unhelpful. We observed in some cases staff who just thrived on the challenge and others who wished it would go away. For this reason I want to discuss theories that focus on individual factors that motivate people. These are called **content theories**, and theories that say why people make certain choices are referred to as **process theories**.

■ THEORETICAL PERSPECTIVES ON INDIVIDUAL WORK MOTIVATION

Content theories: what do they offer

We are all familiar with Maslow's theory of work motivation which states that work behaviour occurs because people want to satisfy specific needs. The needs are hierarchically structured from lower order needs to higher order needs and once a need is satisfied it is no longer a motivator. Maslow identified five needs. These are:

5 Self-actualisation needs

4 Esteem and status needs

3 Belonging or social needs

2 Safety and security needs

1 Physiological needs

There are two fundamental assumptions here. One is that unsatisfied needs motivate behaviour and secondly that as a particular need becomes largely satisfied it becomes less of a motivator for behaviour. This means that the next need in the hierarchy becomes the stronger motivator. This may well be true some of the time but it is equally true that the motivation may come from a need lower down the hierarchy just as well as one above. In other words people are motivated by different needs depending on particular situations and circumstances. A practical example that every local government trainer is aware of is that the training participants need to satisfy hunger and thirst. It does not matter how well the speaker is appealing to the higher order need of self-actualisation, if they overshoot the lunch break by half an hour other needs become paramount. One can observe it in the increased number of people who shift positions or the absence of questions, or exits from the room.

The **assumptions** we might as managers formulate from such a theory can be outlined as follows:

■ people are motivated by social needs and gain a sense of identity through relationships with others

■ people are motivated by physical and security needs

■ people are responsive to and highly motivated by peer groups, this is even more important than financial incentives and work controls

■ people will be active and responsive to management if their social needs for acceptance are met

The **implications** for managers are

- people are more important than the task
- people are motivated if they belong and feel accepted at work
- people can be motivated by group incentives

A good local government example of an application of this approach was used by a City Council wishing to keep the contract for household refuse collection. Staying competitive meant there was no opportunity to offer monetary incentives to increase productivity, so management focused on the social approach to motivation. The team aspects of the job were emphasised, workers were given smart uniforms and more discretion about how to tackle the job. The work teams knew the standards expected and the time allowed for completion, but were then encouraged to decide how they thought the route and households should be covered. The City Council won the bid and has kept the refuse collection in-house against competition to this day. I used this short example because often the hierarchical nature of local government militates against any thought being given to the social and relationship aspects of some jobs. This we see very commonly in the divide between administrative and professional jobs and between junior and middle positions in the hierarchy. Without wishing to be too negative or to overstate the case we do find pockets of management in local government based on a very different philosophy from what can be broadly termed the social approach.

Broadly speaking the rational economic approach to motivation holds that people are motivated by economic incentives; they can of course behave in an irrational way and be unpredictable. This means that as managers we need to display authority and control; these are more important than concern over the feelings of employees. Managers who adopt this approach are likely to do a lot of *telling* about how tasks should be undertaken, rely on monetary incentives to improve performance or seek to tighten control mechanisms. This approach can be applied to part-time staff, the majority of whom are women, in a very negative way. Often part-time staff are described as only working for the money and therefore not requiring any induction or skill development training. We also can see it applied to lower grade posts, to posts that are considered highly routine. Elements of it may be found also in new operational units that have resulted from competition.

Currently in local government we have an increasing number of operational units which are considered either cost centres or business units or profit centres. They all have one thing in common: an interest in the bottom line financial figure. Their managers often speak the perceived language of competition, conversations are interspersed with reference to business plans, marketing strategies, customers and the need for the unit to break even or make a profit. Where the rules allow these managers also talk about staff receiving extra monetary rewards for a good year. This is the rational economic manager in operation: a deep concern with the here and now of the unit. Decisions are primarily based on how will it effect the figures rather than the person. Of course I am exaggerating, and we do not find many such managers in operational units. If they were in the majority it would be a problem, as over-concern for the bottom line can mean that the question how to maintain long-term high performance gets ignored. It is equally true that operational unit managers speak of maintaining quality of service to customers, understanding their competitors and developing staff so that they can respond to the demands and see future trends.

David McClelland (1971) has developed an interesting theory of work motivation which he states is rooted in cultural experiences. His research showed that people had about twenty needs that motivated behaviour. However, McClelland concentrated his research on three particularly strong needs: for achievement, affiliation and power. Like Maslow he believes that needs motivate people to behave so as to satisfy that need. McClelland is interesting for managers because his work has concentrated on finding ways in which managers could develop the ability of others to achieve. Achievement motivation theory proposes that people are motivated according to the strength of their needs and that people's behaviour differs according to the strength of their particular needs. The amount of a need you have is seen as being the result of your childhood, personal and occupational experiences and the type of organisation you work for. The needs are in themselves complex:

1 *The need for achievement* People who have a strong need for achievement, as you would expect, derive satisfaction from achieving goals. They prefer immediate feedback on their performance. They display a preference for working independently, which gives more control over the task, and success or failure is clearly related to their efforts rather than those of others. High achievers do not choose extremely difficult goals, They prefer goals which are either too easy or too difficult to attain. They go for the moderate but challenging goals. High achievers like to discuss acceptance of goals rather than have them prescribed by the boss. They are less motivated by money and more by the need to achieve. However, they often see a good salary as an indicator of acknowledgement of achievement

2 *The need for affiliation* People who are high in this need derive satisfaction from interpersonal interactions. These individuals like to have a good psychological understanding of work colleagues. This is especially true of people they work with on tasks.

3 *The need for power* People who are high in this need derive satisfaction

from being in control of situations and people. Their satisfaction comes from being in positions of power and influence. The power however is directed towards achieving organisational goals and is exercised on behalf of others, rather than for dominance reasons.

McClelland's work sounds realistic and reflects the way we think of ourselves and others. The results were generated by a self-perception projective technique administered to working individuals. The technique in question is a Thematic Apperception Test (TAT). This method presents subjects with different pictures or objects or stories and asks them to state what these mean to them. The problem comes with who interprets the responses and how much researcher bias effects the results. Interpretation is certainly more of an art than a science. People do display behaviours which can be equated with the need for power, achievement and affiliation. Whether one is consistently dominant over the others and influences work behaviours more than other needs remains as yet unproven.

McClelland has conducted extensive research on how to use training to increase high achievement in those individuals who do not register as high achievers. The four main findings are:

- Ensure that employees receive regular feedback on their performance. Feedback serves as a reinforcer and a modifier of task behaviour

- An organisation should have good role models that staff would wish to emulate

- Explain to staff how high achievers accept themselves as individuals and seek job challenges and responsibilities.

- Seek to ensure that employees set themselves realistic goals which they can attain to build their confidence of achievement.

You can see some of these findings being applied in local authorities on Induction Courses where the Chief Executive and other Chief Officers make inputs about the authority. In this way Senior Officers are clarifying how they see their roles and responsibilities and at the same time acting as role models for a future generation of Senior Managers. All four findings are incorporated in more structured coaching schemes especially for new employees, although a view as to their individual achievement need has not been taken. Nevertheless the employing organisation is showing the newcomers how it wishes them to perform and giving them the extra support in the early days.

A major element of McClelland's work has been a concern for matching individuals' motivation patterns to the needs of the organisation. A specific example would be that a social worker may find that her or his dominant need is for achievement. Research has shown this motive to be inappropriate for this type of work (Kolb and Boyatzis, 1971). We can take this one step further and observe the changes that have taken place in Social Services Departments as a result of government legislation. Community care and the purchaser–provider split has for some Social Service departments meant a concern with managerial values such as managing the budget or the provider market. Where these concerns appear to dominate in a department over client or people considerations we can observe and hear high levels of disengagement with the perceived managerial objectives.

One other content theory that has caused a high degree of controversy but remains very popular with practising managers is Herzberg's Motivator–Hygiene theory. On the basis of unstructured interviews with accountants and engineers Herzberg concluded that job satisfaction and job dissatisfaction were conceptually different factors caused by different phenomena in the work environment. This means that some factors contribute to job satisfaction and others can prevent dissatisfaction but not be sources of satisfaction. He called one set of factors **motivators** and the other **hygiene**.

Motivators, when present, cause job satisfaction and are related to the nature of the work itself. So people experience positive feelings about the content of the job and these in turn become linked with factors of achievement, recognition, responsibility, possibilities for growth and advancement. You can see these factors are internal and directly related to the job.

Hygiene factors when not present cause job dissatisfaction. These are related to company policies, supervision, interpersonal relations, salary, job security, fringe benefits, working conditions. These factors relate to the context of the job, are external and directly related to the job.

Herzberg (1987) believes that despite cultural differences hygiene and motivators affect employees similarly around the world. Data from Alder and Graham (1989) in USA, Japan, Finland, Hungary and Italy support this view. This showed that 80 per cent of the factors that lead to job satisfaction for US workers could be attributed to motivators. In other countries the range was 60 to 90 per cent attributable to motivators: in Hungary, for example, it was 78 per cent.

Equally hygiene factors contributed highly to why workers were dissatisfied with their jobs, ranging from 65 to 80 per cent across the sample. Despite the fact that the theory has been criticised extensively on research grounds, it remains popular with practising managers chiefly because it offers a range of familiar terms and factors which offer suggestions to managers about how they might motivate their staff. For example local government has over the recent years increased its range of fringe benefits, such as car leasing, relocation allowances, in a positive move to look at dissatisfaction. In today's climate of uncertainty and change with Local Government Review and white collar CCT the importance of hygiene factors cannot be ignored.

From a manager's perspective the content theories discussed above suggest that certain work-related factors activate the motivational process. They offer frameworks for managers to consider when tackling motivational issues. What they do not do, however, is to say why people choose a particular option. This is what process theories concentrate upon.

Process theories what do they offer

I wish to discuss two process theories chiefly because process theories ask us to think about the internal cognitive processes which people use to choose one action rather than another. Two in particular are useful to the work environment. These are Adams's equity theory and Vroom's expectancy theory.

Equity Theory is based on the assumption that individuals are motivated by their desire to be treated equitably in their work relationships. If this is so then there are four important considerations:

- Person — the individual for whom equity or inequity exists
- Comparison other — any group or individual used by Person as a referent with regard to inputs and outcomes
- Inputs — characteristics individuals bring with them to the job; these may be ascribed, such as ethnicity, sex, age, or achieved, such as education, experience etc. They are also subjectively perceived by the person
- Outcomes — those things that individuals receive from the job such as pay, promotion, fringe benefits. These are subjectively perceived by the person

The motivation to act comes after the Person makes his/her own comparison of inputs with outcomes. They then compare it with their perceived ratio of inputs and outcomes of relevant others in the same or similar situation. Inequity is defined as the perception that a Person's job input/outcomes ratio is not equal to the inputs/outcomes ratio of the comparison Other.

A good example of this can be seen in problems with performance-related pay schemes. Often in local authority schemes people at the same level are given similar amounts of monetary reward on the basis of achieving targets. One can observe what happens when within a working group, an individual works harder, completes more tasks and achieves her targets. At the end of the year all workers in that group receive their performance-related pay even if targets have not been achieved in entirety. Where this has occurred the scheme very soon loses its incentive value for individuals who have worked according to the aims of the scheme. It is equally possible that the person who receives the bonus and who has not performed well may be motivated by guilt or social pressure to work harder to reduce the imbalance between their inputs and outcomes in comparison to the work group as a whole. What equity theory highlights is that inequity causes tension within the individual and between individuals. This means that people employ strategies to reduce the tension when inequity is perceived. These are:

- The Person may increase or decrease inputs or outputs relative to those of Other
- The Person may subjectively distort perceptions of their own or Others' inputs and outcomes
- The Person may decide to compare themselves with a different Other
- The person may leave the situation

Equity theory tells us that people like to be treated with fairness whether it is in relation to pay and conditions or to procedural fairness (that is, how decisions are made). If we think about the tension that can be caused if the staff member asked to cover the phone during lunch-time feels this is inequitable. In efforts to improve economy, efficiency and effectiveness many local authorities have restructured in major ways. This has often lead to staff being redeployed or made redundant. The manner in which this has been dealt with is of utmost importance to the future motivation of staff. In the case of redundancies, if those who remain feel decisions have been equitable they are more committed to the authority or department than if the decisions are seen as inequitable. Equally redeployed staff will soon lose any sense of relief at not being made redundant if they find themselves unable to perform in their new post due to lack of knowledge or skills.

Expectancy Theory: again we can see that this theory concentrates on people's thought processes. One of the basic assumptions made in expectancy theory is that people think quite a lot about doing things before they actually do them. People are seen as rational individuals who consider what they have to do to gain the rewards they value and whether the required action is worth the reward. Therefore motivation to behave in a certain way is determined by:

- the outcomes the person sees as desirable
- the persons belief that these outcomes can be attained

In other words individuals are making decisions about the amount of effort they are willing to make in performance terms to achieve a desirable objective. Alternatively people also decide to avoid doing things that will lead to undesirable outcomes. The theory recognises that individuals have different expectations, that decisions are most often situation-specific and dependent on how a decision can meet their needs. For example an individual may have competing desirable objectives, one work-related the other home- or recreation-related; as we know these can clash.

■ WHAT CAN MANAGERS DO ABOUT SEEKING EFFECTIVE WORK PERFORMANCE?

If you reflect on what these theories are suggesting and on what you see in terms of their application in good practice in your own and other local authorities you can see that they combine into an approach to designing jobs and tasks. These theories have been in the management literature for several decades; in fact they were the basis of the Hackman and Oldham studies in the 1970s and 80s which have had an enormous influence on the way in which work is designed and structured for effective performance. One of the conclusions we can draw from the motivation theories discussed is that work itself has an influence on motivation, satisfaction and performance. Therefore if we look closely at how jobs and tasks are designed we can perhaps increase motivation and achieve improved performance. The reason we would wish to tackle motivation from the job factor point of view is because people are complex and make decisions based on both internal needs and external factors in particular work situations. Cognitively individuals will consider a multiplicity of factors before making decisions about work behaviour. This leads us to take a pragmatic approach and focus on changing external factors, which could create a favourable work environment conducive to people's work preferences.

Hackman and Oldham's **Job Enrichment Characteristics Model** is research-based. It suggests that there are five core characteristics which every job should have. These core characteristics influence three critical psychological states which in turn influence several desired personal and work outcomes. (see Figure 5.1 for graphic representation of the model).

Simply put, Hackman and Oldham's model suggests that internal rewards are obtained by individuals when:

they learn (knowledge of results)
they experience personal responsibility (experience of responsibility)
they have performed well on a task that they care about (experienced meaningfulness of work).

The more these three psychological states are present in a job, the more satisfied individuals will feel when they perform. The model recognises the

Core Job Characteristics	Critical Psychological States	Personal and Work Outcomes
Skill variety Task identity Task significance	*Experienced meaningfulness of the work*	High internal work motivation
Autonomy	*Experienced responsibility for outcomes of the work*	High quality work performance High satisfaction with the work
Job feedback	*Knowledge of the actual results of the work*	Low absenteeism and turnover

Individual Differences

● Knowledge and skills

● Growth need strength

● Satisfaction with contextual factors

Figure 5.1: Job Characteristics Enrichment Model
Source: J.R. Hackman and G.R. Oldham (1975) 'Development of the Job Diagnostic Survey', *Journal of Applied Psychology* (Vol.60 No.2. pp.159-70)

individual nature of motivation by stating that performance will be affected by knowledge and skill, the desire for achievement, affiliation and autonomy (growth need strength) and satisfaction with contextual factors.

The five core job characteristics are absolutely critical to the model. The following definitions clarify the essential requirements:

- **Skill variety:** degree to which the job involves a number of different activities that use different skills and talents

- **Task identity:** degree to which the job requires the completion of a whole and identifiable piece of work.

- **Task significance:** degree to which the job has impact on lives or work of other people within the organisation or the external environment

- **Autonomy:** the degree to which the job provides substantial freedom and independence and discretion to an individual in scheduling work and in determining the procedures to be used to carry it out.

- **Feedback:** degree to which individuals in the work process obtain direct and clear information about the effectiveness of their performance.

According to the model all jobs need to be high on at least one of skill variety, task identity, task significance, but must include autonomy and feedback. Hackman and Oldham suggest five principles for enriching jobs and redesigning work:

Forming natural work units: increasing ownership of the task by putting together interrelated activities. This can increase the core dimensions of task identity and task significance. We see this in formally recognised units such as group, section or department. Managers who form and reform project groups for specific tasks are conscious of the effect on staff of undertaking specific projects.

Combining tasks: by combining several related aspects skill variety and task identity are increased. An example from local government would be a senior officer permitting the officer who wrote the report to present it to committee . The report writer is using presentation and political skills as well as the skills of report writing.

Establishing client relationships: making the relationship between the producer of the good or service and the receiver/client closer. Current local government examples would be placing central staff from Personnel or Treasurers into service departments, the Citizen's Charters initiatives, consultation exercises with clients around issues like local management of schools or infrastructure projects and community development initiatives.

Vertical loading: the intention here is to close the gap between the doing and controlling aspects of the job. Examples would be letting staff select own work method, choose hours of work, inspect their own work, or participate in decisions affecting their job or the organisation. This increases an individual's autonomy, accountability and responsibility. In local government we see this principle in schemes of management delegation for the newly formed operational units. It involves management being moved to an arm's length position from the parent department.

Open feedback channels: here the emphasis is on how the job itself can offer feedback directly to the person so that they are continually reminded of the quality of their work. This can be built into a lot of jobs in the sense that checking for completeness can be undertaken by the job holder against standards.

■ WORDS OF CAUTION

While a considerable amount of research supports the ideas described above it is equally true that other researchers question the relationship between motivation, satisfaction and performance. Nevertheless it is generally recognised that in Britain we have quite some distance to go in exploring work contexts that lead to employees experiencing increased satisfaction at work due to environmental conditions such as quality circles and flexible patterns of work. However even more important than those reservations is the need to be aware that at least four organisational systems within local government can affect the likelihood of the successful implementation of any job enrichment plan:

1 *The technical/service system* In local government the type of service you are operating in will of course affect what kinds of jobs you might consider suitable for increasing in autonomy. There are in many instances statutory requirements which would not permit this, supervision in social services being an example. Equally some jobs, like Chief Officers or technically sophisticated posts, are so naturally enriched that nothing could be gained by job enrichment. The reverse is also true. Some jobs are very difficult to enrich.

2 *The personnel system.* Personnel systems can constrain job enrichment by creating very formalised job descriptions that are rigidly defined and limit the flexibility one has in changing job duties. This can involve union negotiations where very traditional agreements are in place.

3 *The control systems* Budget procedures, accounting systems, management information systems and control systems can limit the complexity and challenge of jobs.

4 *The reporting system* The managers and supervisors to a large extent determine the amount of autonomy and feedback that subordinates will receive. This in the final analysis is a crucial issue especially in tall hierarchies where individual status is often measured by the size of your budget and the number of people for whom you are responsible. Management delegation schemes have had uneven patterns of effective implementation, some schemes being blocked by particular managers who are reluctant to delegate. Success has often had to be achieved at the highest level by Chief Executives making it clear that the schemes are a high priority and must be effectively implemented.

If the above are not constraints in your authority there are some other factors to be taken into account when considering job enrichment. These are the necessity of having in place supportive schemes of training and management development and career development planning which reinforce the need for discretion, responsibility and accountability (see Chapter 8 for full explanation of this point).

■ IMPLICATIONS FOR YOU AS MANAGER

This chapter in an effort to understand what motivates people to behave in certain ways in work situations has discussed several theories of motivation. These were divided into two broad categories of content theories and process theories. The content theories stress the internal processes within individuals that energise them to particular behaviours. These theories focus on the internal needs of individuals and attempt to specify what needs motivate behaviour. The process theories on the other hand are more descriptive and seek to explain why people make certain behavioural choices. Here we discussed expectancy and equity theory. The link was then made between those theories and how they have been applied to job redesign/job enrichment in the job characteristics model. Examples of the practical applications of these theories in local government contexts were given.

Here are some questions for you:

1 How do you seek to motivate your staff? Are you a social relations manager or a rational economic manager or a blend of the two?

2 Do you think the distinctions between motivation, ability and performance are important?

3 How do you cope with the view that motivation is an individual phenomenon?

4 Do you think group working can enhance the performance of individuals?

5 Do you think management role models are important motivators?

6 Do you give staff autonomy and feedback where possible?

7 How important do you think an individual's expectations about outcomes are in motivating behaviour?

8 Do you always consider the equity element before you make management decisions?

9 Which of Hackman and Oldham's five characteristics of job enrichment would be easily identifiable in the work environment for which you are responsible?

10 Do you offer staff achievement opportunities through their work experience and or through training /management development?

11 Do you set performance targets jointly with staff?

12 Can you think of circumstances within local government which would make Herzberg's hygiene factors more important than his motivators and vice versa?

13 Do you agree with McClelland's view of the need for power, and how do you respond to people operating from a power basis?

References

Adams, J.S. (1963) 'Toward an Understanding of Inequity', *Journal of Abnormal and Social Psychology* (67, pp.422–36)

Alder, N.J. and Graham, J.L. (1989) 'Cross Cultural Interaction: The International Comparison Fallacy', *Journal of International Business Studies* (Fall, pp.515–37)

Hackman. J.R. and Oldham, G.R. (1975) 'Development of the Job Diagnostic Survey', *Journal of Applied Psychology* (Vol.60, No.2, pp.159–70

Herzberg, F.I. (1987) 'Workers' Needs: The Same around the World', *Industry Week* (September, 21, pp.29–32

Kolb, D. and Boyatzis, R. (1971) 'The dynamics of the helping Relationship' in D. Kolb, I. Rubin and J. McIntyre (eds) *Organisational psychology.* Prentice-Hall, Englewood Cliffs, N.J.

McClelland, D. C. (1971) *Motivational Trends in Society.* General Learning Press, Morristown, N.J.

Maslow, A.H. (1970) *Motivation and Personality.* Harper and Row, New York

6

Performance appraisal and management

Key points

◆ An authority-wide approach to performance management which links Members' policy objectives to authority and departmental objectives is the context in which individual performance appraisal finds greatest clarity.

◆ It is through individual performance appraisal that managers can develop clearly the target aspects of tasks in conjunction with the supportive relationship aspects of the appraiser/appraisee roles. Both aspects are essential to effective work outcomes.

◆ Managers require a clear view of what issues they are seeking to address by introducing a performance appraisal scheme. These objectives should influence the choice of scheme.

◆ The individual skills required for successful performance appraisal must be addressed by action learning training during the implementation stage.

■ INTRODUCTION

Appraising performance can be a very sensitive issue. Appraisal has become a more central management tool as authorities have moved from line/command structures and role cultures to more flexible structures and task cultures. This chapter refers in the first instance to the debate about whether to measure personality traits or work performance. Generally in Britain the focus of appraisal is on work performance. The growth of interest in local government in performance management is discussed with the attendant skills that this requires from managers. Performance management is shown to be the context in which appraisal takes place. The point is made that appraisal systems have different core purposes which affect the way appraisal is conducted. Four types are discussed and an assessment of their intended benefits is made. The key factors that need to be considered in the introduction of schemes are outlined. Finally the chapter focuses on the individual skills required in the appraisal process.

■ BACKGROUND

Employee appraisal in the broadest sense has had an important historical hurdle to overcome in the UK. In the 1950s and 60s the dominant approach to appraisal was personality-trait based procedures, coupled with a graded rating system approach. A typical list of traits on which an individual would be appraised focused on Leadership, Honesty, Integrity, Intelligence, Decisiveness, Warmth, Conscientiousness, Reliability, etc. It was McGregor in America (1957) who first raised doubts about this conceptual approach. This was followed by an empirical study in Britain by Rowe (1964) which revealed that managers were very reluctant to use personality-trait based type schemes. There followed several key studies in America and Britain, among them Maier (1952, 1958) Randell (1972) Anstey *et al.* (1976). In essence these and other studies raised several key issues on the methods adopted in appraisal. It was suggested that:

- a concentration on job related activities and behaviour is the best substitute when quantitative job measures are not possible
- the skills of interviewing and the training of interviewers are essential parts of the process and this skill should be a management prerequisite.
- the evaluative nature of appraisal in terms of individual personality is counter-productive. A problem solving approach to the exchange was recommended
- appraisal contained within itself three elements, reward, potential and development
- action learning by role play was the most appropriate method for training in appraisal skills.

The growth of interest in appraisal in the 1960s and 70s in the UK meant that several surveys of actual practice were undertaken. The Institute of Personnel Management commissioned three studies, two by Gill in 1972 and 1977 and the third by Long in 1986.

Collectively these studies covered 954 companies. The main trends noted were:

- a move away from trait approaches to both organisational and individual development
- about 40 per cent of companies in the 1970s did not appreciate the importance

of training staff in appraisal skills. This had reduced to 22 per cent in the 1986 sample

- the emphasis in the schemes was on measuring current performance
- appraisal for performance-related pay had in 1986 remained at about 40 per cent of the schemes
- failure of schemes was often attributed to lack of interviewer skills, over-elaborate paperwork, lack of consultation, failure to consult, and lack of commitment from the top.

As Randell observed the trend in Britain was towards a person-centred, skill-based approach. Against this background in 1983 Mr R. G. Brooke, the then Chief Executive and Clerk of West Yorkshire Metropolitan County Council and Chair of the working group which produced the booklet 'Appraisal of Management Performance' wrote:

Local government has been concerned to develop the management skills of its officers for some years. Few local authorities have, however, used performance appraisal as part of their management development scheme. There is a sharp contrast between the wide use of performance appraisal in the private sector and its relative neglect in local government.... There is now a great deal of interest in formal appraisal systems in local government and many local authorities are introducing or thinking of introducing them.

■ PERFORMANCE MANAGEMENT AS THE CONTEXT FOR APPRAISAL

One of the interesting developments in the last fifteen years has been the growth of interest in the whole area of performance management in the public and private sector. While many might struggle to give a clear definition of performance management most would agree that we can identify certain factors that are likely to be present in organisations that say they use performance management. In local government terms we would express them as follows:

- mission statement and strategic policy priorities at authority level which inform all that follows
- departmental and unit objectives, business plans

- an emphasis on quality services and performance-related pay
- a focus on the performance of senior managers
- performance targets expressed in terms of outputs and accountabilities
- management development, training and learning targets
- performance appraisal processes
- Chief Executive and Chief Officer presentations utilised as a means to inform and communicate performance requirements
- a performance review system at organisational and departmental levels

From the above we can see that performance management seeks to integrate the strategic policy objectives of the authority with individual and group goals. There is a focus on methods of goal setting, performance appraisal, and reward systems. Performance management aims to reinforce the work behaviour of individuals and groups towards the strategic direction of the authority. The Local Government Management Board undertook a major survey of performance management and performance-related pay in the summer of 1993. They reported an overall response from 279 authorities; almost half of the authorities had introduced formal performance management systems. In this survey performance management was defined as the setting of corporate, team and individual targets, and their later assessment to see if they had been achieved (*Local Government Management*, Winter 1994). The same survey indicates that 25 per cent of the authorities in the sample had adopted performance-related pay. Within these authorities' PRP schemes, the trend was to cover less than 50 per cent of staff, with indications that this would remain the practice. The following example is a Performance Contract for a Chief Executive.

PERFORMANCE CONTRACT (1 APRIL 1992–31 MARCH 1993)
Job Title: Chief Executive

Key Responsibilities	Objectives
1. Build and maintain constructive working relationships between Members and Officers	*Initiate arrangements for improved dialogue between Leader, Members, CMT and DMTs, with a view to more effective decision-making in the Council

Cont'd

---

2. Support members in the development of policies, programmes and budgets, and maintain the machinery for doing so	Review the means for committee monitoring of progress of programmes against plan Initiate means of reducing the amount of paper going to Members, leading to a review of delegations to officers Explore the scope for using Policy Panels more fully in the Council
3. Deliver services to the public within the plans and to the standards determined by Members	Establish with Members whether there are sufficient measures of public satisfaction and whether Members' standards of service are sufficiently defined Take forward the (x) objectives for customer care and satisfaction
4. Account for the effective and proper use of the Council's resources within agreed budgets	Agree with the Finance Director respective roles and responsibilities in this area Ensure that an early warning system is in place to identify potential overspends at an early stage
5. Develop the structures, skills and working methods of the Council to meet the requirements placed on it	Carry through the current change programme, ensuring that it and other initiatives are properly co-ordinated Complete the delayering of the top structure Get the right structure in place for the TSO and PSO
6. Lead, direct and motivate the Council's employees so that they can contribute fully to its work	Support Chief Officers, particularly in Education and Housing, in managing difficult transitions in their departments Put in place a programme to build leadership skills in the Council Implement the goals for CMT itself as agreed at (x) Prepare a plan for communicating the vision of the Council more effectively to staff Build the findings and conclusions from the staff survey into plans for internal communication and improved leadership

Cont'd

7. Maintain national and local external relations which further (y) interests	Maintain contacts and relationships which give (y) early warning of national development e.g. on CCT and enable (y) view to be heard Pursue as necessary with colleagues (y's) interests and physical development and maintain effective communications with the local business community

From the above example you can see that such a performance contract has four key elements:

1 Each individual has a performance contract setting out her/his contribution in a specified period
2 The contract clarifies where the individuals' key responsibilities lie
3 It states the contribution expected through the objectives
4 The contract typically covers a year and needs to be reviewed regularly for relevance

■ INDIVIDUAL SKILLS INVOLVED IN PERFORMANCE MANAGEMENT

Research by the LGMB and others shows that authorities who are committed to performance management tend to speak about outputs, accountabilities, key responsibilities, key result areas, delegation, customers, freedom for front line staff, freedom for line management, the need for internal service providers to be responsive to operational requirements, the importance of structures and systems. What does this say about the skills that managers need, to achieve success in such a system? Here is a list which I think demonstrates in terms of the amount of skills, the high demands we now place on our managers. The list assumes that outputs are king and key in performance management.

Managers require the skills to:

■ integrate outputs with management information systems
■ integrate outputs with appraisal
■ integrate outputs with job evaluation

- integrate outputs with job specification
- integrate outputs with budgets
- integrate outputs with team building
- integrate outputs with organisational design
- integrate outputs with organisational learning

Central to this approach is the need to redefine the traditional approach to job descriptions. There needs to be some way of expressing in what areas a person is expected to achieve results/outputs, which outputs are to be measured and where the person has authority to act. Once a manager has decided this they must then seek to ensure that each individual considers how he or she is going to make his/her own discrete contribution to 'making a difference'. This is a difficult area; many people in organisations never find the means of making and taking their role so that they do make a unique contribution. This is something managers must be aware of; one aspect of the manager's role is to create a work environment where staff know that they can exercise the authority that is delegated to them. Clear job definitions coupled with clear autonomy and responsibility are building blocks for performance management.

Individual or team focus

It is in this area that we find a dilemma as to whether it is best to have an individual or team focus for setting key result areas. In essence the manager is seeking maximum contributions and hoping to avoid any overlap or underlap in individual contributions due to confusion as to the exact details of who is concentrating on what. The argument for a team approach is that you recognise the interdependencies and visualise the organisation as a series of interlocking teams. Within a team no person's key result areas should overlap or underlap with other team's members. Overlap is when two persons are accountable for the same output. Underlap is when no one is accountable for a particular output. To ensure that key result areas complement those of other managers, each manager must see that their key result areas include those of their subordinate managers. Equally a manager's key result areas are included in those of their superior. Thus managers are members of their superior's team, and if they have subordinates, are the top person of their own team. The aim is to seek to improve the performance of all team members by setting key result areas, measurement and authority in an open forum. This increases the possibility of more effective communication, greater commitment and results in a more holistic approach. A few authorities have developed a team approach to deciding such outputs and they report high satisfaction with the results.

In considering whether to adopt an individual or team focus it is useful to ask yourself where you think your authority is in terms of organisational development. Performance Management depends on more than setting a system in place. A team approach is likely to be more successful where the organisation has the following features:

- values which reinforce openness, fairness, equity, customer quality, autonomy, accountability and responsibility
- a climate which values staff
- a climate where learning is encouraged
- systems that reinforce collaboration
- a decentralised structure
- staff with good interpersonal skills

There is no easy formula for deciding which way is best but the introduction of a team approach generally requires an outside facilitator at the inception and high scores on the above features. What we are much more familiar with in local government is the individual approach to appraisal and, more recently, setting that within the wider framework of a performance management framework.

■ A TYPOLOGY OF FORMAL APPRAISAL SCHEMES

From the discussion of the background and context of appraisal, we can see that performance appraisal is a broad term used to cover a wide range of procedures. These usually involve a manager or supervisor giving direct evaluation and feedback of individual or work group performances. In local government it is useful to consider schemes in terms of their main purpose. This means that we have four main types:

1 Personnel management type schemes

These are usually driven by a central personnel department. The purpose is to collect comparative data on organisational members to assist in making decisions about such items as salary increments, promotions and regrading. The comparative data is seen as a means of ensuring some equity and consistency over sensitive career decisions.

We know, in organisational behavioural terms, that managers experience difficulties with these schemes. The centrally controlled and defined predetermined criteria are an obstacle in creating a sense of individual ownership of the scheme by departments and individuals. While the concept of predetermined criteria is meant to increase the objective nature of the interaction, the individual being appraised generally believes it to be highly subjective. The use of rating scales generally receives a negative response from those asked to administer them. People react to being labelled a four or a five or a two. In addition, research shows that rating scales are subject to the central tendency error where the vast number of evaluations drift to the centre of the scale where it is nice and safe. The tendency also is to judge on past performance, often with implications for the future in the sense of salary and promotions. The future is not explicitly addressed. Local government on the whole has not introduced many schemes that are so centrally defined, largely because diversity within each local authority is recognised and because the interest in appraisal stems from a concern with effective organisational performance. Equally personnel in local government has never concentrated on centrally defined career and succession planning due in no small measure to an emphasis on equal opportunities in recruitment and selection and the separate professional career structures within authorities. The rest of this chapter will concentrate on the implications of the remaining three categories.

2 Appraisal schemes aimed at improving current performance

These schemes are an integral part of a structured and planned management process, which would typically include strategic priorities, departmental plans and business plans. The prime purpose of these schemes is to compare the current performance of individuals against an established standard. Performance appraisal in this sense is seen very much as part of an overall process of performance management which is rooted in a plan for organisational performance.

Managers involved in the scheme have to contextualise the job of the appraisee within the overall performance management framework of the department. The ethos of the scheme is one of joint planning and discussion about job performance. The performance will be clearly outlined in terms of targets and performance criteria. It is absolutely essential that targets are jointly agreed and that the manager is prepared to play a clear role in supporting the achievement of targets where required. This means the manager and appraisee working out what organisational obstacles or constraints may exist that would impinge on attainment of desired outcomes. The process is seen as continuous and agreement is reached as to when and how evaluation should take place.

3 Appraisal schemes aimed at management development and training

The purpose of these schemes is to integrate the development aspirations of individuals with the chosen direction of organisational development. The idea is to develop the potential of individuals in line with the needs of the organisation. These schemes look forward to future growth and development and seek to anticipate future needs. These schemes can assist local authorities to identify 'skills gaps', particularly in times of changing demands. It is not uncommon to see the Management Charter Initiative Competency Framework used to identify the skills and knowledge required in the local government environment.

Managers operating this kind of scheme require a counselling type of approach, as well as clear views about the skill and knowledge requirements of job holders, so that the identified individual development needs are supportive of overall organisational needs. Managers have to weigh the costs of long-term development needs with short-term needs and the suitability of the individual seeking development. These kinds of schemes have a longer history in local government and grew out of a tradition of concern with possibilities for in-the-job development. We can associate the skills of coaching, mentoring, job secondments and special projects with developments in this area.

4 Performance-related pay schemes

These schemes aim to give a clear monetary reward to individuals, based on their achievement of set work targets. The schemes seek to relate some proportion of pay not just to individual output but also to other indicators, such as quality, achievement of objectives, effectiveness and contributions to team work. These schemes operate within the context of an overall approach to performance management.

Managers involved in these schemes are seeking to reinforce the direction and objectives of their authority/department/division/business unit by rewarding job behaviour which clearly achieves work targets. In behavioural terms the giving or withholding of a reward, not the least a monetary reward, is a delicate issue. Nevertheless schemes soon loose their credibility if everyone is rewarded when it is obvious that not all have succeeded. The withholding of reward has been more clearly a part of Health Authority schemes than local government schemes. One also has to address the problem that targets differ in degrees of difficulty across the authority. There may be no clear evidence for this but subjective perceptions can be a powerful obstacle to successful negotiation of targets. Managers sometimes have to contend with a reluctance by staff to admit to failure in achieving a target that is linked to monetary reward. On the other hand there is the view that the small amount of money involved in the incentive does not really motivate people to achieve the targets. In addition managers are sometimes seen to get the incentive, while others feel they have done the work. Chief Officers on performance-related pay often find problems with targets agreed at the beginning of the year. A change of focus leaves them with the dilemma that to pursue those targets would be counter-productive for the department. Schemes that include target setting must allow time to renegotiate targets for relevance. Where the scheme is focused on the individual this can run counter to other organisational objectives such as team working. One way round this is to have contributions to team working as an appraisal criteria.

■ YOUR ROLE AND FORMAL METHODS OF APPRAISAL

Every manager who is involved or about to be involved in a formal appraisal process needs to address the question; why adopt an appraisal scheme? The very direct answer is that people like to know where they stand in the organisation. From the perspective of the individual this is often never explicitly stated but, revolves around four very simple requests:

- agree with me what is expected of me
- give me the opportunity to perform
- tell me how I am getting on
- support and develop me to achieve my agreed objectives

Following on from that, the individual then has an expectation that she/he will be rewarded on the basis of their contribution. Reward may be interpreted very broadly, as in opportunities for interesting work, new learning experiences, verbal praise, or more narrowly in the sense of clear unambiguous pay or promotion. If I had a pound for every local government officer who assured me that they do this all the time I would be a wealthy woman. The reality is that these basic needs of the individual are not in the majority of cases met by the informal processes of appraisal, due in some measure to lack of a planned structured approach and the infinite capacity of individuals to misinterpret one anothers' conversations. Equally, the formal process of appraisal can fail to fulfil these basic requirements when the scheme tries to address too many conflicting objectives. Hence the impor- tance of an appraisal scheme having clear objectives as in the four types outlined above.

One way of approaching the issue of addressing the requests of the individual appraisee as a manager conducting appraisal, is to think of how you are going to respond to the four requests above. Then you might come up with the following list of areas to be jointly discussed:

- clarify areas of responsibility and performance standards expected/achieved
- identify and discuss areas of strengths and weaknesses
- establish where possible the reasons for success or failure in achieving required standards. Separate out individual and organisational contribution to outcomes
- where cause is within an individual's control, discuss how she/he can share that success with others or be helped to achieve required standards
- develop constructive joint plans to build on strengths and to overcome weaknesses
- demonstrate your willingness to support and the ability of the organisation to be supportive
- if necessary clarify the reward structure
- share information about the appraisee's current position in the organisation and look to future job development.

The list is not exhaustive. It focuses on the needs of the individual and also recognises managerial and organisational needs. Where you place your emphasis will of course be determined by the prime purpose of your particular scheme. For appraisal to be effective it must be clear to the appraiser and the apppraisee that there are benefits to be gained by both parties to the exchange.

■ ORGANISATIONAL BEHAVIOURAL ISSUES IN ANY FORMAL APPRAISAL SCHEME

Research and my own experience of consultancy in designing and introducing appraisal schemes in local authorities indicate very strongly that many of the problems associated with conducting effective appraisal schemes stems from lack of attention to the following areas by the implementing authority/ department/Chief Officer/Manager.

Credibility

Taking an authority-wide perspective, it is essential that commitment to the scheme is clear. This means that the Chief Executive and Chief Officers are all appraised. This is one case where top down is best, appraisal begins with them and moves downwards. This process is further strengthened where the involvement of elected members, meaning the Leader and Chairs of relevant committees, is built into the scheme for Chief Executive and Chief Officer appraisal. The importance of training managers in the appraisal process has to be tackled, all appraisers must participate. This includes the Chief Executive and Chief Officers. Participation does not mean opening the training session and disappearing. It means staying and actively participating in the learning process for the whole designated period. Credibility is further enhanced when all staff have open access to their own appraisal forms on demand during the life of the scheme. This point links to ownership of the scheme.

Ownership

To introduce performance appraisal across the authority it is important to recognise the diversity between departments and to seek to reflect that diversity in the form that appraisal takes within departments. While the decision to introduce appraisal may have been taken at the corporate level, in my experience it works best where each department designs their own scheme within a broad framework of perhaps 'Improving Current Perfor-mance' or 'Management Development and Training'. Where this is not acceptable to the culture ways must be found to ensure the key element of ownership at the operational levels within the organisation. In either circumstances the key word here is consultation. This is no time to designate one person to design the scheme in isolation and then present it for implementation. You may smile, but it has happened. In one particular instance the designed scheme was very well thought through, but staff believed it was imposed. The consultation must obviously include the relevant unions. Local government unions are generally supportive of schemes that offer opportunities for individuals to develop within their jobs. They do naturally like to be fully consulted when the scheme is first mooted and to be well briefed as the scheme develops. Most importantly, the people who are going to operate the scheme, either as appraisers or appraisees, should be consulted. The following are the main areas where staff wish to make a contribution:

- establishing the system's purposes and objectives
- ensuring that the appropriate information is available to support the proposed system, for example departmental plans, business unit plans
- ensuring that the procedures of the system are fair and that they permit the appraisees' views to be adequately represented

- considering how the actual appraisal exchange should take place. This covers: philosophy of the system, timing of appraisal cycle, appraisee preparation, appraiser preparation, amount of paper work, how performance is to be measured, how information is to be stored and used, access to appraisal information

- planning for the training of all appraisers and ensuring that all appraisees are fully familiar with the system before the first cycle

A consultation period may seem to entail both time and effort but it really is vital in seeking to demonstrate to senior and line managers as well as to staff who will be appraised, what the potential benefits are. Successful schemes all are characterised by credibility and ownership, otherwise appraisal becomes just a form-filling exercise driven by the need to complete the cycle and get on to the next task.

Here are two extracts from a County Council's Planning and Transport Department's Staff Appraisal Scheme following a consultative approach to the design of its scheme:

Introduction

Staff appraisal is part of the annual cycle of activity in the department which is all about managing its resources effectively. Every year during the autumn and winter period the Department prepares its budget for the following financial year, with all the problems and politics that entails. At the same time, group managers are preparing their business plans for the following year; they are setting out what they hope to achieve with the financial resources available to them. The Senior Management Team has the difficult decisions to make about overall objectives and priorities, when, inevitably, choices have to be made.

Apart from money, the Department's other major resource is its staff whose salaries account for 80 per cent of the administrative budget. The Department is, in effect, the sum of its parts and four hundred individuals all have their part to play. It follows, therefore, that careful attention should be given to the performance and development of this resource and that is what the appraisal process is all about.

Everyone in the Department is affected by the process. The Director is appraised by the Chief Executive and in turn appraises his Management Team. The appraisal process then follows the management chain through group managers to every individual member of staff.

Cont'd

Benefits to the organisation

Appraisal links every individual's contribution to the business plan

Staff are clear about what is expected of them and are better motivated as a result

Development needs of individuals are identified systematically

Training resources are allocated to meet the organisation's business needs

Good quality information is available about staff performance

Benefits to the individual

Uninterrupted discussion with your manager

The answer to the question: how am I doing?

The opportunity to agree forward work programme

Being able to put your own views forward

Being able to discuss your achievements, ambitions and future development

The introduction places the scheme within an overall framework of performance management and clearly states that everyone from top down is included in the process. The benefits remind appraiser and appraisee of the potential and intentions of the scheme.

■ THE INDIVIDUAL SKILLS INVOLVED IN APPRAISAL

It needs to be said that even when every attention has been paid to the planning, consultation and design of appraisal schemes, problems can still arise due to the absence of the required skills. People can learn these skills, and they learn best by an action learning method. Appraisal training should always involve the trainees in role play exercises, which ensures they undertake the role of appraiser, appraisee and the role of listener/observer during the training period. We know that appraisal schemes can differ as to their purposes and content; nevertheless there are some core skills that are appropriate. In very simple terms the appraiser needs **self awareness, awareness of others, knowledge of the appraisee job, awareness of the organisation and awareness of the wider environment outside the authority and how to access it.**

As a manager it is very useful to consider the appraisal interview as a perceptive, meaningful, purposeful conversation. If we take the three key words of perceptive, meaningful and purposeful we can define some of the skills we are seeking.

Being **perceptive** in appraisal situations means an awareness of the other person's experiences. Appraisal does not take place in a vacuum. It may be affected by authority positions, external pressures, new work systems, personal experiences etc. Individuals differ in the ability to be direct in conversations. Being perceptive means picking up cues and aiding others in expressing their true position.

Being **meaningful** in appraisal requires the ability to create empathy. This is done most easily by genuineness, that is, being yourself, not just playing a role, being aware of your own feelings and thoughts, communicating verbal and non-verbal cues that match the appraisee's.

Being **purposeful** in appraisal conversations means that you have to concentrate very carefully on skills that do not come very easily to us. We are socialised to think that a conversation means a lot of talking, and some of us are guilty of only waiting to interrupt the speaker with what we had decided to say before he/she even started. Being purposeful means developing the skills of **active listening**. There are two parts to this skill. One is the external ability to stay silent, while giving non-verbal messages of interest e.g. good eye contact, nodding, open posture, etc. The internal side is the ability to consider the information you receive in an objective manner, not to make assumptions, ask what the appraisee means or feels or knows. This kind of exchange shows that you are considering the perspective of the other person in a purposeful manner and reinforces the value of the appraisal. Some managers struggle with the idea of not being in charge of the interview. But being in charge is not equated with speaking the most. A good appraisal interview typically would mean that the appraiser only spoke twenty to thirty per cent of the time. One of the great skills in appraisal that falls under being purposeful is how well the appraiser can fit his/her agenda into the agenda of the appraisee. Remember the purpose of appraisal is to permit the appraisees to state their concerns and hopes, while the manager makes a clear statement about expected performance. The aim is to create an environment where appraiser and appraisee can discuss achievements and expectations.

Appraisal interviews come in all shapes and sizes but they all need the following:

- *Plan* The appraiser needs to consider the objectives, the degree of formality, the approach, the environment, the time and the place
- *Orientation* There is no best way to conduct an appraisal interview. Each

individual adopts his or her own style as he/she becomes skilled

- *Sequence* Every interview needs a beginning, where the purpose is established, a middle when information from both participants is exchanged and an end where future actions are agreed
- *Awareness* Good appraisers use time effectively, they do not let the appraisal drift on nor do they cut it short
- *Learning* Following an appraisal the appraiser should ask himself/herself why did it go well or not so well. Did I deserve the help I received from the appraisee or was I to blame for lack of empathy?

Knowing local government's fondness for acronyms you can remember this as POSAL. You will have noted that under 'Orientation' I stated that no one style is best. In essence it is good to be flexible. Individuals differ and will require different approaches from you depending on the circumstances. It is equally true that, through training, many local government officers develop a problem-solving approach to the exchange which transcends a particular management style, such as benevolent, authoritarian, consultative or partici-pative. The problem-solving approach is very much in keeping with schemes where joint action needs to be agreed by appraiser and appraisee. It is believed to encourage ownership.

■ IMPLICATIONS FOR YOU AS MANAGER

Managers seeking to improve performance have a range of approaches they may consider. In essence the manager needs to be quite clear about the purpose she/he wishes to address when considering the different approaches. The key to any approach is wide consultation with all the stakeholders during the formulation and implementation of the chosen system. In addition the manager must demonstrate commitment to the process by ensuring that the skill-training implications of any scheme are fully addressed. The manager's full involvement in the training process is essential.

References

Anstey, E., Fletcher, C. and Walker,J.(1976) *Staff Appraisal and Development.* Allen and Unwin, London
Fletcher, C. and Williams, R. (1985) *Performance Appraisal and Career Development.* Hutchinson, London
Gill, D., Ungerson, B. and Thakur, M. (1973) *Performance Appraisal in Perspective.* IPM, London

Gill, D. (1977) *Appraising Performance: Present Trends and Next Decade.* IPM, London

Local Government Training Board (1983) *Performance Appraisal and Identification of Potential.* LGTB, London

Long, P. (1986) *Performance Appraisal Revisited.* IPM, London

McGregor, D. (1957) 'An Uneasy Look at Performance Appraisal', *Harvard Business Review* (35, 3, pp.89–94)

Maier, N.R.F. (1952) *Principles of Human Relations.* Wiley, New York
          (1958) *The Appraisal Interview.* Wiley, New York

Randell, G.A. (1972) *Staff Appraisal.* IPM, London

Roberts, G. (1994) 'Performance Figures', *Local Government Management* (Winter, pp.32–5)

Rowe, K.H. (1964) 'An Appraisal of Appraisals', *Journal of Management Studies* (1:1, pp.1–25)

7

Management development and the individual

Key points

◆ The authority which ignores management development neglects the human resources which are the most valuable asset of any authority.

◆ Management development means individual and organisational development, organisational development being the context for the relevance of individual development.

◆ Authorities and managers require an integrated approach to management development.

◆ All managers should take an active part in defining the development needs of the organisation and individuals. This kind of review process encourages organisational learning.

■ INTRODUCTION

This chapter makes the point that management development for the individual employee must take place within an overall strategy for corporate management development in an authority. In this way the contribution to be gained from individual development is clearly directed to benefit both the individual and the organisation. A corporate approach can address the concerns that exist in different authorities in relation to management development activities. You may recognise some of these in your own authority.

In some authorities there is a lack of an integrated planning process for management development. This means that the activity receives uneven attention across the authority. Since the prime purpose of management development is to ensure that individuals can contribute to effective organisational performance, this is a matter for concern. In terms of equity it is desirable that all staff have a clear view of the range of management development opportunities available to them and how they may access them.

Pressures for change, brought about by legislation, require new ways of working and the development of new roles and priorities. Examples in local government would be Local Management of Schools in Education, the Griffiths Report on Social Services, Compulsory Competitive Tendering and the introduction of business units and cost centres in many authorities. The training and management development implications of these and other changes need to be considered so that staff have the opportunity to acquire the skills needed for effective performance.

Local government has a strong requirement for discipline-based specialists with professional qualifications such as social worker, educationalist, treasurer, planner and lawyer. These discipline-based skills are essential if the local authority is to deliver a quality service. Equally in today's world of local government where privatisation and contracting out are the operational norm, the delivery of quality services to the community requires managerial expertise. Authorities and managers need to find ways to enhance professional and managerial development. There is often a lack of shared learning within an authority in relation to management development activities.

This chapter wishes to address these issues but before doing so it is important to clarify a number of key terms which are central tenets of this chapter.

- *Management* embraces those activities which all managers undertake irrespective of the discipline/professional context in which they occur. The demands, or requirements, made on a person in a management job may be considered the functional requirements of that job. Functional requirements of management jobs can be described in terms of five basic functions: **planning; organising; controlling; motivating;** and **co-ordinating.** Each of these functions can be examined in terms of the various tasks and skills that constitute that function. The performance requirements associated with each function will differ according to the level on which it is undertaken in the organisation.

- *Management development* has two core elements: personal and organisational development. Development as an idea embraces both the outer reality of environment and 'organisational goals' and the inner reality of the 'self'. The dictionary defines the word development as 'the act or process of growing, progressing, or developing.' The idea implies change and continuity; it seems only logical that the aim of management development is to create an environment in which individuals have the opportunity to consider and agree ways of achieving personal and organisational goals. Organisational development implies a process of examination of strategies, structures and systems to evaluate their appropriateness to cope with the existing internal and external environment. If change is present in either of these environments this may call into question the current strategies, structures and systems.

Management development is a continuous interactive process in which individuals' job experiences, career progression and opportunities for learning are undertaken in the specific context of organisation development.

- *Corporate management development* implies management development for the authority as a whole, the corporate body. This should not be taken to mean that management development is defined by the Centre. What is required is a corporate strategic approach, where Members and Chief Officers review the strategic plan for the authority and incorporate a review of the human resource skills needed to achieve it. Then corporate management development initiatives are planned to provide the skills to manage the strategy. Management development needs are derived primarily from the strategic plan of the authority. In this way the needs of individual departments are met within the corporate framework. All management development activities (corporate, departmental, unit) should be the result of an interactive process between client and provider. This means that clients are involved in defining, approving and reviewing the management development activities of the provider agencies, be they internal or external.

Background

One of the primary objectives of management development is the creation of conditions where the potential of employees will be realised and their commitment to the success of their contribution to the authority secured. This potential is taken not merely to include the capacity to acquire new skills and knowledge, but also to release a source of ideas about how the organisation's operations might be better undertaken.

There is evidence to suggest that training and development activities have an effect on competitiveness and economic performance in business organisations. The most important comparative study in Britain was undertaken by the Institute of Manpower Studies and the National Economic Development Office in 1984. These have been followed by the Handy Report (1987) and Constable and McCormick's *The Making of the British Manager* (1987). Both have emphasised the paucity of training and development in comparison to international standards and the need to develop good practice in management education, training and development. More recently the Local Government Management Board (LGMB) has strongly taken up this theme in two publications: *Squaring up to Better Management: A Survey of Management Development in Local Authorities in England and Wales*

(1990) and *Achieving Success: A Corporate Training Strategy* (1991). These two publications are of direct relevance to any authority considering a way forward for management development.

All the above publications have one common overriding theme. Organisations, public or private, which concentrate solely on responding to the challenges placed upon them by undertaking a reassessment of their resources such as finance, structures, marketing and technology to the exclusion of their human resource are missing the vital ingredient. The LGMB 1991 publication puts it thus:

> Yet, ultimately, the most important resource of the authority is its staff. The delivery of a high quality, timely service depends upon their commitment, flexibility and knowledge. Training and development is therefore crucial: playing a vital role in preparing and enabling staff to achieve the objectives of the authority.
>
> *Achieving Success*, p.1

Underpinning this statement is the firm belief that training and management development must be seen as an **investment in people and not just a cost to be cut at the first sight of budgetary constraints**, which can be a big temptation in this new world of competitive decentralised units in local government.

■ A STRATEGIC APPROACH TO CORPORATE MANAGEMENT DEVELOPMENT

Corporate management development must be integrated into the wider planning in the authority. This is seen as crucial. These activities must no longer be peripheral to the achievement of organisational objectives. In this way the human resources of the authority become a vital component in corporate planning, training and development. They are seen as being able to make an important contribution to the achievement of service objectives. To succeed, a demand for increased management development activities must command the participation and support of the most senior levels of the authority. The belief that management development is important needs to come from members and officers. The Local Government Management Board's publications (1990 and 1991) highlight the following core elements of good practice on the part of local authorities, other public sector bodies and private sector companies as essential to an integrated approach (Northampton County Council; Hertfordshire County Council; Surrey County Council; Childline; and Jaguar Cars):

1 Management development needs to be derived primarily from the strategic plan of the authority. In this way the needs of individual departments are met within the corporate framework.

2 Management development needs to function at three levels: organisational, departmental and individual.

3 Management development and professional development need to progress in parallel streams.

4 Management development must strike a balance between individual needs and organisational requirements.

5 Management development must have the commitment and active involvement of senior officers

6 Adequate resources must be allocated to management development and the temptation to cut this allocation needs to be resisted, even in difficult times.

7 The design of management development programmes and the selection of learning methods must take into account the nature of managerial work.

8 Decisions about management development must take into account the needs and capacities of individual managers.

9 People assigned to management development should be among the most able in the authority with the potential to go to the top. They should receive adequate education and training to prepare themselves for the task.

10 Management development should be systematically reviewed and evaluated to establish its contribution to individual and organisational performance.

To meet the above list of requirements it is apparent that roles and responsibilities need to be clarified. Consideration also needs to be given to the structures and systems of training and management development needed to fulfil such an approach.

Roles and responsibilities

In essence what research into the experience in local government has shown is that successful corporate management development requires a direct input into the planning process. This has been achieved by authorities in several ways. Examples are given below:

1 The chief officers are clearly responsible for training and management

development with the management development specialists facilitating and supporting that role.

2 Training and management development is given a corporate role, with that person responsible for focusing management development on the achievement of corporate and departmental objectives in consultation with Chief Officers, while the responsibility for implementing the training and development policy is given to Chief Officers.

3 The Chief Executive and the head of corporate support services hold regular meetings with the personnel officer and the corporate management development officer to discuss and review training and development as they relate to current and future trends.

4 Whatever option is chosen there must be clear responsibility and accountability with the top levels of management. This then must be translated to all levels of management so that managers are clear that they have individual responsibilities to develop their staff, in a manner which will ensure that individuals have the capacities to cope with the present job and are being prepared for future foreseen changes in line with the direction of the authority.

Every strategy must have a structure to support its implementation. It is to this that I now turn.

■ A STRUCTURE CONDUCIVE TO CORPORATE MANAGEMENT DEVELOPMENT

Developing effective management potential is seen as common to all management jobs irrespective of their professional location. The context and level in which people manage may be different but there are core functions which every manager needs to perfect. In addition there exists a wide range of management skills which particular managers may be called upon to acquire depending on situational circumstances. It is these broad areas of activity which present authorities with the possibility of becoming organisations where learning is shared across departmental boundaries.

To be organisationally effective, management development needs analysis has to be linked to management and strategic planning. Such an analysis provides the organisation with information as to its present and future requirements. This will mean looking forward to create a vision and being clear about direction, purpose, mission and task. Management development audits establish where the organisation is now, in terms of existing skills and abilities. Clarity of vision establishes where an organisation wants to be. The gap between these two is a measure of the organisational development need.

The following steps give an outline of how to build corporate management development into the corporate strategy of the authority:

- Members establish council aims and objectives

- Strategic plan for the authority
  (Management development specialist identifies the level of investment and resource available for management development)

- Corporate goals and objectives of authority
  (The management development specialist identifies the management development requirements of the above and plans for them)

- Departmental plans: targets and key tasks
  (The management development specialist identifies the management development requirements of the above and plans for them)

- Business/service plans: targets and key tasks
  (The management development requirements of the above are identified and planned for)

- The management development specialist ensures that a formal evaluation and review process of management development which includes the participant, the line manager, peer group, client department/corporate client and provider, are undertaken

The management development strategy for an authority/department/unit needs to be fully integrated into the strategic direction of the authority, thus identifying the human resource requirements for effective performance. An important element of this is a clear framework outlining the training and management development activities in the authority to which people have access. This leads directly to the need for the authority and its managers to have clear plans so that management development needs may be integrated with them. Management development programmes are the implementation details of the strategy and plan. Management Development has matured in the last ten years with a deeper understanding and appreciation of the needs of the adult learner. This has been coupled with the awareness that management training must be relevant to the current and future work experience of the learner. This means in effect that management development activities have to focus on the present and future demands of the workplace.

■ A LEARNING ENVIRONMENT FOR ADULTS

Learning is not about behaviour changes that occur due to the personal maturation process. It is about a change in behaviour that is reasonably permanent and grows out of experience. For adults whose reservoir of experience is so much greater, any behaviour change must occur as a result of a deeper and more meaningful experience than that of a child. Thus, some of the theories of learning that have been applied to children may not be as effective if applied to the teaching of adults. The adult learner is a somewhat different species from the child learner, and this should be reflected in the design, method and delivery of programmes.

Malcolm Knowles has coined the phrase **andragogy** for his system of adult learning, which is different from the theory of **pedagogy** used for learning in the young. It is a **process** model and is based on the assumption that, as an individual matures, her/his need and capacity to be self-directing, to utilise experience, to identify one's readiness to learn, and to organise learning about life problems, increase steadily from infancy to pre-adolescence and then increase rapidly during adolescence.

Andragogical theory is based on four assumptions that distinguish it from pedagogy or traditional teaching methods.

1 Concept of the learner
2 Role of learner's experience
3 Readiness to learn
4 Orientation to learn

These have implications for the manager:

1 Motivation of the individual is an intrinsic process so that they are self-directing. The role of the manager is to create a learning environment that harnesses these intrinsic drives and not an environment that suppresses them.

2 Self-directed individuals need support. The role of the manager is to recognise when the individual needs support and to provide support either personally, or using group members or management development providers.

3 Wherever possible the experience of the individual must be tapped. To deny a person's experience is to deny that person. The probing of experience from people with different backgrounds so that they may learn from each other is one of the fundamentals of action learning which has been applied with notable success in management education.

4 The participative method utilises members' experience for the benefit of others, including the manager. According to Kolb (1984) it is only by having an experience that people begin the cycle of learning. Involvement in an experience ensures that the span of attention is widened so that individuals learn more. Knowledge and skill are acquired and also certain emotions are felt that can be a powerful way of changing attitudes.

5 The content of the management development activities should be a contract between the learner, the manager and the trainer or the manager/trainer. This meets the learner's needs for relevance. The involvement of the learners in deciding the content of management development activities increases commitment because they part-own the decision.

6 Where knowledge is imparted with the individual in the passive mode, there should be ample opportunity to reinforce learning by varying methods. Reinforcement is a vital part of the learning process and methods used should vary according to subject material and individual learning styles. Variety stimulates and makes the learner more receptive.

To summarise, according to Knowles, the andragogical model is a **process model**, not the **content model** that has been employed by traditional education. The andragogical manager/tutor is a facilitator, a consultant, a change agent, who prepares in advance a set of procedures for involving the learners in the process of:

1 establishing a climate conducive to learning
2 creating a mechanism for joint planning
3 diagnosing the needs for learning
4 formulating objectives and therefore content and process which will satisfy these needs
5 designing a pattern of learning experiences
6 conducting these learning experiences with suitable techniques and materials
7 evaluating the learning outcomes and re-diagnosing learning needs

The process model does not ignore content. Rather the emphasis is on providing procedures and resources for facilitating the learner's acquisition of information and skills. This ownership by the participant of the objectives and content increases the commitment, harnesses the learner's intrinsic motivation; this is a powerful way of influencing attitudinal change.

David Kolb (1976, 1984) and Honey and Mumford (1986) have also concentrated on how adults learn and the nature of the differences that exist between people. They suggest that there are four distinct stages in the learning process and that each individual has a preference for a particular style of learning. Kolb developed his experiential learning theory, seeing it as an integrated process in four main stages. Learning begins with the here-and-now experience termed concrete experience. This could conform to existing views or contradict them. This experience is followed by a collection of data and observations or reflections about that experience. Next come a continuation with an analysis of the data, when we begin to conceptualise and commence the internalisation process of what we have learnt from the experience. The final stage is when we modify or alter our behaviour. This is a stage of experimentation and testing the new knowledge or concepts to see if they work in practice.

These four distinct stages provide key concepts for consideration in the design and training methodology of management education activities for adult learners. Management development providers who subscribe to this philosophy, seek creative ways of building on participants' current experience, then extending their horizons to consideration of alternate concepts and strategies. A very interactive **learning-by-doing** style is adopted. Extensive use is made of such methods as game playing, role plays, field visits, work-based projects, problem-solving based on live organisational concerns that involve content and process issues. Let us look more closely at the issue of content and process as it is incorporated into the idea of the Management Charter Initiative (MCI standards) and how it could be used by you as a manager.

The idea of individual competence and competency

Staff throughout the authorities, because of the pace of change, have found themselves grappling with the intricacies of a range of **new areas of competence** from business planning to marketing to customer care to quality assurance. I use the term **area of competence** as it is used in the Management Charter Initiative, referring clearly to an area of work at which a person is competent. This area of competence has its own 'standard'. For example 'recruit and select personnel' is an MCI standard. It is subdivided into elements shown in Table 7.1, and each of the elements has performance indicators against which competencies can be judged.

Elements	Define future personnel requirements; determine specification to secure quality people; assess and select candidates against team and organisational requirements

Table 7.1: Examples of MCI standard

There is a particular sense in which the word **competency** is used. Here it refers to the dimensions of behaviour that lie behind competent performance. This is the person-related sense of the word for which the word competency is reserved in the MCI. For example 'showing concern for excellence' is a personal competency, while the example in Table 7.1 is an area of competence. In this second sense, competency refers to one of the sets of behaviour that a person must display in order to perform the tasks and functions of a job with competence. Examples of competencies in this second sense can be taken from the UK's Government Information Service (GIS):

Solution finding:	Thinking through a problem and translating it into practical terms; generating practical ideas for a solution; evaluating the solutions by gauging outcomes of action; ensuring a result is achieved; accepting compromise and improvising if necessary; taking on problems; coming forward with ideas.
Rapport:	Being able to talk to people of all levels; getting others to talk; forming good working relationships; seeing the situation from the other's view; adapting to the other person; building on others' ideas; helping others in crises; keeping others/seniors informed; being sensitive to others' views
Entrepreneurship	Spotting, creating and exploiting opportunities, e.g. for financial savings, revenue generation, sponsorship, free publicity, media coverage

Table 7.2: Examples of GIS Competencies

In the view of GIS, members need the competency labelled 'Solution-finding' in order to perform tasks like devising a publicity campaign (area of competence).

It is important to realise that **areas of competence** and **person-related competencies** are derived from two different bases of analysis. Areas of competence are derived from functional analysis based on an analysis of job functions. They tend to be quite specific as the MCI standards show. On the other hand analysis of person-related competencies proceeds in the opposite direction. It starts from specific types of behaviours, and groups these types of behaviours under the competency. The goal is to cluster into dimensions the behaviours that indicate the high performer. The label for a dimension is simply the best wording to capture the common denominator of the behavioural indicators. One cluster of behaviours might be:

- Identifies priorities in the agenda
- Includes key people in the discussion
- Consults concerned parties
- Anticipates resource requirements
- Listens to all views
- Manages own and others' time
- Demonstrates fairness but moves items on

It might be decided that 'Chairperson skills' best captures this cluster. The process is from the indicators to the label, and not vice versa. It is vital that a list of competencies is flexible and capable of reflecting the changes in the organisation's direction. The list must reflect the best estimate of what the future will require of people, and it must be kept under review.

Managers who keep the idea of personal competency (process) and areas of competence (content) separate in their minds can use them as a tool for assessment and development. It is important for managers to appreciate the different roles for areas of competence and competencies in individual development. In particular, areas of competence are much less useful than competencies for development feedback to staff or learners engaged in management development activities. For example, one of the elements in the unit of competence in the MCI Standard 'Initiate and implement change and improvement in services and systems' is *negotiate and agree the introduction to change*. If someone is not good at negotiating and agreeing, they need to know why. As the elements stand all that can be said is that they fail to negotiate and agree introduction to changes in services and systems. But why? What are they doing wrong? How can they improve? The answer will lie in a combination of the competencies they need to acquire. These are the dimensions against which people should be assessed for readiness or potential to move into jobs, and against which people should be appraised.

They are also the dimensions upon which people should be **developed**. Before exploring more fully how people may be developed it is important to consider the context in which this development will take place.

■ PROVIDING A FRAMEWORK FOR DESIGNING MANAGEMENT DEVELOPMENT ACTIVITIES WHICH RECOGNISES DIVERSITY

Most importantly the **values** of an authority influence all that they do. While it is quite common to have them explicitly expressed they are always implicitly present in any approach to management development. It is clearer to state the values that inform the choice of organisational strategy and the view of personal competences and areas of competence. Strategy is of course directly related to the purpose and direction we set ourselves. The chosen strategy has implications for organisational design, systems and skills. In short it provides the essential operating environment in which all staff demonstrate their personal competences and areas of competence. Performance appraisal, development reviews and/or a skills audit help us to define or redefine where we wish to place our emphasis when developing staff. The benefit for managers in having a clear framework is that this view can inform the processes of recruitment, induction, review of performance and promotion. The framework can engender in staff a feeling of belonging to one organisation. This is especially crucial in times of constant change and increasing fragmentation in local government. The framework will also inform the design and delivery of the numerous targeted management development activities run within an authority. The interactive nature of the diagram seeks to demonstrate the dynamic and interrelated nature of the relationships, the grounding of management development within the practical world of work and the need for constant review.

From the diagram shown in Figure 7.1 you can see that management development programmes need to be understood in the widest possible sense, so that we move away from the idea of management development and courses meaning the same thing. This has arisen because of the past tendency in local government to isolate the training and management development function on the periphery of local authorities, away from senior management and councillors. In the following headings I explore in more detail the ideas behind the elements in Figure 7.1.

Provider/client activities

Planned management development ought to be based on a clear, formal view of the content of a person's job and the context in which that job is

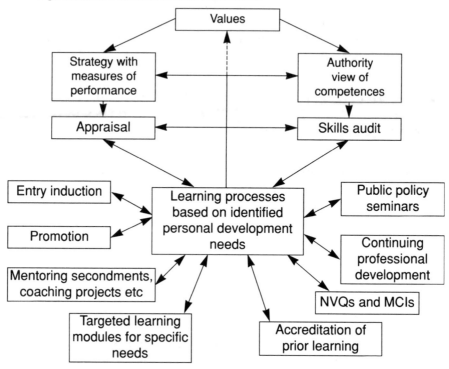

Figure 7.1 Towards a learning environment

undertaken. This means clarity of job purpose and clarity about unit/departmental/corporate objectives.

In my view it is essential to move away from the pattern of behaviour where the provider of management development programmes receives a loose specification of what is required and then seeks to supply the demand. It is not surprising that such delivery vehicles are often rejected by clients. We need clear ownership on the part of clients, be they individual, unit, departmental or corporate.

The other way to design programmes/activities is in close collaboration with the client (the word 'client' is used to represent those who define a view of the needs/requirements of the purchaser of the programmes/activities). In this situation the client specifies their requirements and the provider seeks to meet those needs in a consultative manner. This kind of specifically designed management programme is a very interactive process between provider and client and has a strong element of consultancy from the provider, and problem-solving on the part of the client organisation. It involves the following steps in planning and delivering:

1 Initial contact involves negotiations as to the scope of the consultancy, e.g. length of time, level and number of participants, depth of investigation, etc.

2 Familiarisation and investigation of client issue.

3 Providers' identification and assessment of personal and organisational issues.

4 Providers' first thoughts as to the content and process of the management development programme based on the results of (2) and (3).

5 Negotiations with the client as to the actual content and process of the management development programme. This would include an agreement to implementation of outcomes from the programme and methods of evaluation of the programme.

6 Providers design and run the programmes (this could be in-house or external).

The strengths of such an approach lie in its interactive processes. It engages the client and provider in the management development process. Proposals are more likely to be 'owned' by individuals who have helped to generate them. The approach is suitable for management development at different levels in the hierarchy and it is capable of taking account of individual and organisational development goals. It links clearly with the idea of the learning organisation, where responsibility for learning is shared across the work environment. My own authority uses this approach with its internal provider and with external providers.

The following is a practical example from Warwickshire Planning and Transport Department who were introducing a performance appraisal scheme for their department.

The Personnel officer initiated contact with the internal provider, 'The Learning Company'. Following discussions it was agreed that the way forward would be to investigate jointly the best approach in collaboration with an external provider. A joint investigation and identification followed and a proposal was submitted for consideration and consultation. Further discussion led to a contract for the training of all appraisees in performance appraisal. There were three crucial stages to the contract. **Stage one** consisted of a jointly run process and content two-day workshops on appraisal which allowed for the practising of both process and content elements. **Stage two** is of course the putting of these skills

Cont'd

into real use in the department. **Stage three** is the agreement by the Planning and Transport department and the providers to review jointly the implementation of the scheme. In this way the training and the real practice will be evaluated in the practical world of work. Evaluation will include contributions from superiors, appraisees and the appraisers who were involved in the process.

The authority as a learning organisation

Here we can see that provider and clients are developing a culture where learning is valued and the results of learning, when fruitful, are incorporated into the world of practice. The idea of a 'learning company' or organisation has been gaining currency in the U.K. This calls for an organisation to be so aware of its organisational environment, that it can recognise the need to adapt and change to meet changing requirements. Finding such organ-isations has not been easy, but the idea is certainly gaining currency: 'The excellent companies are learning companies' (Peters and Waterman, 1982, p.110). So we can see that learning organisations are those in which training and management development have become intrinsic to the organisation. Attwood and Beer (1990) make the very valid point in reviewing the Mid Essex Health Authority's experience of becoming a learning organisation for effective performance, namely that management development must be supported by other organisational systems.

Creating a learning environment

The diagram has outlined a range of activities which recognise different approaches to learning. It is important that there is a set menu for staff to choose from as in table d'hôte, while always making it clear that à la carte is available for consultation. What follows is a sample of ideas that can be made available to the adult learner. The manager's role in this is crucial—she/he may not be an expert in management development but ought to know what is available and how to access further information.

Increasing professional and vocational qualifications are being accredited to the NVQ framework which emphasises competence in the workplace. This emphasis on competence has a range of integrated accredited programmes for the development of managers at the different stages of career development.

The following Table 7.3 illustrates the stages:

NEBSM	NVQ3	MCI (Supervisory)
CMS	NVQ4	MCI I
DMS	NVQ5	MCI II
MBA		

Table 7.3: Table of Accredited Courses

People may choose different routes but it is important to have a picture of what is available or expected so individuals can make informed choices about what they wish to pursue. (*Key to above table:* NEBSM=National Examination Board for Supervisory Management, NVQ=National Vocational Qualifications, CMS=Certificate in Management Studies, DMS=Diploma in Managment Studies, MCI=Management Charter Initiative. MBA=Master in Business Administration.)

Senior management development activities

The aim here is to cover a range of managerial issues, personal competences and areas of competence. An example could be Public Policy Seminar Series for Members and officers addressing policy and managerial issues that are current in your authority. Titles might include: Markets and Quasi Markets in the Public Service; The Experience of Public/Private Partnerships, The New Public Management, Quality Assurance and Quality Management. Women into Management, White Collar CCT, The Implications of Local Government Review.

New Developments

These could emerge as a result of a management skills audit or in response to internal or external changes . The main point here is that the environment has to be scanned for developments. The new developments might include such topics as a need for increased financial awareness, new skills in cross-boundary working and a need to increase officers' abilities to work with communities (perhaps a greater number of officers are being required to develop political sensitivity skills and with CCT being introduced in new areas this will call for increased expertise).

Mentoring, secondments, projects networks etc.

Very often when different groups of staff are asked the following or similar question, 'Given the range of possible management development activities it would be useful if you could indicate five activities you have experienced and which you found effective?' the dominant responses are experiences related to Mentoring, Coaching, Special Project Work, Secondments and Networking. These answers recognise the fact that attendance on courses and seminars and identifying competencies can only be part of an authorities approach to management development. Managers must seek imaginative ways of developing staff at work. Accreditation for prior learning is one method of realising the value of on-the-job experience as are learning contracts. Sharing your knowledge of particular areas of local government with others is another way of developing staff. There is in fact a wide range of activities to choose from some of which have been highlighted.

Management development activities
Secondments, projects, task enrichment, coaching, mentoring, job swaps, development with the job, individual learning agreements/contracts, resource centre where people have access to learning material, seminars and short courses (in-house or external), sequence of programmes for junior, middle and senior managers. Provider/client-designed management development activities.

Equal opportunities
Looking at the implications of equal opportunities across the board, on-service delivery as well as employment can be a powerful way of facilitating the development of greater equality of opportunity through the achievement of organisational objectives. **The concept of identifying competencies can help to eliminate stereotypes about qualifications and experience and further enhance an authorities/department or units progress towards equality.** Responsibility for progress cannot be the preserve of a group of enthusiasts outside the mainstream of the management structure.

■ SYSTEMS WHICH SUPPORT MANAGEMENT DEVELOPMENT

Performance appraisal

Within the framework and philosophy outlined so far, the manager may choose to use an existing performance appraisal scheme or devise a system of **Individual Performance Review (IPR).** The design of an IPR system permits individuals to identify their own training and development needs and to consider how they may meet their own needs and how these fit with the organisational objectives. The system also seeks to ensure that managers and subordinates participate in a debate about training and development. Thus it is hoped to avoid the situation where training and development are marginalised to some central resource where needs are met in a very mechanistic manner, often most inappropriately. Many training surveys show that the most senior personnel have acquired the highest proportion of the organisation training budget, even when there is a clear need for middle and lower level training. Equally the choice of training programmes can be very arbitrary with resultant effect on the individual's ability and motivation to learn. This is very closely linked to the lack in many authorities of a planned approach to career planning. The argument has often been used that because individuals can choose to apply for their next promotion, somehow this reduces the need to plan careers. However an essential proportion of a manager's job should be the development of their staff.

Career planning/management

In local government we can distinguish several main career directions. They are manual, clerical and administrative; technical/professional; functional management; and general management. Each of these may have separate streams. The questions for career management are:

- How do people progress up a ladder?
- How do people move from one ladder to another?

Moving vertically is natural and easy; most people understand their boss's job or the next level on the rung of a ladder. Many people's vision in local government is limited to that also. To be competitive today we need to develop people who are flexible, with a broad range of skills to offer. Movements across functions are valuable in building up experience, and one of the weaknesses of the self-development approach to career growth is that the individual usually finds it difficult to engineer such movements. Since this idea is about planned movement of people, one has to think about the mechanisms for movement: not just the processes of appointment but management development schemes which facilitate career development. This could be:

- departments encouraging planned job secondments to build careers
- an integrated series of management development programmes for different levels of supervision and management
- the development of an authority-wide approach to the career development of clerical and administrative staff

When authorities and managers look ahead, it is not much use to think of one step only. It is the same for individuals, they need a career aiming point—a position to aim for in five to seven years time—with its characteristic profile of knowledge, skills, attitudes and experience. Then people can analyse the gap between where they are and where they would like to be, and make a plan to close that gap.

An integrated approach to management development requires links between the individual, the manager, the unit, the department and the authority. There is of course a need to evaluate the outcome of what is undertaken in the areas of management development. The key here is to think of management development activities as cyclical processes.

■ AN IMPACT MODEL OF EVALUATION

The ultimate purpose of evaluating management development programmes/ activities for the manager is to ensure that the learning processes are effective in producing the desired and expected outcomes. However, management development does not take place in a vacuum and is only one resource input among many within a total organisational system. The impact model of development looks at management development in the context of the organisational system as a whole.

The model views management development as being part of the fabric of transforming inputs into outputs. Management development stands as a contributor among other organisational activities involved in the process of achieving outcomes. Any management development activity which cannot be seen in this way by Members, officers and management development specialists probably ought not to be undertaken. Management development should be capable of being evaluated for effectiveness in terms of the differences it makes to those involved.

The impact model is an approach to evaluation which assesses effectiveness in terms of what people involved say it is about and what they want to achieve. The basic premise is that if the major players in any management development initiative are demonstrably getting what they previously stipulated as a real need, then this is a good indicator of success. Thus the criteria by which effectiveness is assessed are the defined expectations that individuals stated in the first place.

There is no doubt that there are many different ways of seeing things. The various players in any situation will have different views, perceptions, based on their underlying values or beliefs, and on their place in the organisation. The impact model recognises this multiplicity and most importantly accepts that the perceptions of all major players in the management development activities have a rightful place in the evaluation process.

■ IMPLICATIONS FOR YOU AS MANAGER

This chapter has made the point that individual management development must take place within an overall corporate framework. The role of the manager is crucial at the level of needs analysis, delivery and outcome review. The manager needs to be involved in constantly refining and defining the development process at the level of both organisational and individual development. The manager has a role to play in encouraging a climate where learning is understood and accepted as a key aspect of the management function. Leadership in this way demonstrates that management development is a collaborative and co-operative process, that it goes beyond the limits of the instructional and training model. The manager through management development is seeking to improve the overall performance of the system in which she /he operates.

References

Attwood, M. and Beer, N. (1990) 'Towards a working definition of a learning organisation' in M. Pedler, J. Burgoyne, T. Boydell and G. Welshman (eds), *Self Development in Organisation*. McGraw Hill, London

Constable, R. and McCormick, R.J. (1987) *The Making of British Managers: A report for the BIM and CBI into Management training Education and Development*. BIM, London

Handy, C. (1987) *The Making of Managers: a report on management education, training and development in the USA, West Germany, France, Japan and the UK*. National Economic Development Office, London

Honey, P. and Mumford, A. (1986) *Using Learning Styles*. 2nd edn. Peter Honey, Maidenhead

Knowles, M.S. (1980) *The Modern Practice of Adult Education: From Pedagogy to Andragogy*. Follett, Chicago

Kolb, D. (1976) *The Learning Style Inventory*. McBer and Co., Boston

Kolb, D. (1984) *Experiential Learning*. Prentice- Hall, Englewood Cliffs, N.J.

Peters, T.J. and Waterman, R.H. (1982) *In Search of Excellence*. Harper and Row, New York

8

The management of change

Key points

◆ Understanding the process of change is essential to its effective management.

◆ Change is not a linear discrete process in which an organisation moves neatly from one stage to another.

◆ Managers of change need to recognise clearly that organisations are clusters and coalitions of interest that engage in both integrated and disparate sets of activities.

◆ Change initiatives often disturb the implicit psychological contract individual employees have with the organisation.

■ INTRODUCTION

The preceding chapters have made it obvious that local government has experienced huge changes in the last fifteen years. What made the changes so dramatic was the awareness that they were being externally driven. It was not always the case that the changes were seen negatively but rather that local government was being asked to respond to a steady stream of new legislation and/or new operational rules. Since 1979 there have been over a hundred acts/bills of Parliament which directly affect local government. The result is that the understanding of the process of change is a prerequisite for the effective manager. Too often in local government, changes have been introduced in a sterile way, leaving staff with a feeling that changes have been imposed or not fully understood. Both of these reactions mean that the desired outcomes of change are not achieved. This chapter takes an organisational development perspective and examines several concepts of change that are influential in how people interpret the change process. With examples from local government, it points to key organisational and individual elements that must be considered by any manager seeking to manage a change process effectively.

■ UNDERSTANDING CHANGE AS A CONTINUOUS PROCESS

Kurt Lewin, a pioneer in the 'systematic study of planned change' (Kanter, Stein and Jick, 1992) in the mid 1940s developed what is now classified as one of the early fundamental classic models of planned change, Force Field analysis. The essential proposition of the theory is that organisations, like people, prefer to maintain themselves in a steady state of equilibrium or balance. As an open systems theorist no doubt Lewin was influenced by the biological concept of homeostasis as it relates to individuals. Lewin suggests that change is brought about by the strength of various forces, internal and external, to the organisation, impinging sufficiently on the steady state to effect a change in strategic and operational norms. Behaviour at any point in time is the result of the two sets of forces. When both sets of forces are equal, behaviour is in a 'quasi-stationary equilibrium' (Lewin, 1947). In order to change the equilibrium one needs to either increase those forces driving for change or decrease those forces (maintaining the current state) by restraining change, or a combination of both. Both driving and restraining forces can be internal or external to the organisation and forces come in various forms, whether it be people, technology, tasks or structure.

Example of driving forces for change

INTERNAL FORCES: Changes in the goals of the organisation, incongruity of personal and organisational goals, presence of innovators, ineffective performance/results, unfavourable organisational climate, resistance to authority and power conflicts between departments/ units

EXTERNAL FORCES: Uncertainty in the environment, changes in political power, economic change, demographic changes, cultural factors

RESTRAINING FORCES:Personal factors such as fear of change and systemic factors such as resources rules and agreements

---

You can see from the above that local government can identify with a huge number of these factors. Lewin suggested that the most successful approach is to work towards reducing the barriers to change rather than increasing the forces towards change because people are complex and the latter approach produces less tension and resistance to change and is therefore possibly a more effective method of making sustainable intervention.

Lewin's model is a simplistic one, viewing the process of moving from one equilibrium to another as consisting of three steps, similar to handling an ice cube.

Unfreezing: this step usually involves reducing the forces within an organisation which are maintaining the organisation's present norms, values and patterns of behaviour. Lewin's theory has been elaborated by Edgar Schein (1985) and others who suggest that for change to occur, unlearning has to take place before new learning can occur, particularly for strongly held beliefs and habits. Unfreezing is sometimes accomplished by information which shows the discrepancies between current behaviours and their effect, in comparison to behaviours desired by the organisation. These ideas are closely allied to the concept of the learning organisation, where the organisation demonstrates the ability to review performance and to consider what is to be learnt from the results of strategic and operational activities. In local government we have many examples of unfreezing. Think back to the days when financial information to service departments arrived in the format preferred by Treasurers. Service departments challenging the cost and appropriateness of central charges and the need for the authorities as a whole to be competitive, led to an unfreezing of procedures.

Changing/Moving: following unfreezing people are open to new information, to help in developing new values and behaviours as a result of changes in organisational structure and processes. Schein suggests that the collection of information for the development of new action plans can take two forms, **identification** and **scanning**. Identification results in information coming from one source, whether it be a manager, consultant or somebody who can exert some form of coercive power. On the other hand scanning involves the use of multiple sources of information. An example of scanning can be drawn from local government where authorities planning the introduction of some new structure or system often seek information or knowledge from an authority which has introduced something similar earlier. Scanning generally requires a lot more effort and time than identification but people are more likely to accept the change when they have been involved in the change procedure.

Refreezing: this step involves stabilising the organisation at the new equilibrium and preventing a regression to 'old' behaviours. To achieve this step changes are often directed at affecting the culture, norms, structures and policies which seek to reinforce the new organisational equilibrium state. This stage often fails because change covers very emotive issues such as values, norms, culture, etc. A number of these issues may be so deep-rooted in the individual, group or organisation that they are at a subconscious level. People's deep-rooted values influence their behaviours. For example if somebody values educational qualifications they may assume that less qualified people are not suitable for promotion. This value often persists despite evidence that individuals are doing very well in the job. A problem associated with values is that they are often hidden or unexpressed. Therefore, subconsciously individuals, groups and organisations conform to their values. These levels do not develop in isolation. They interact and influence the development of one another. So introduction of a change process is a complex cycle. Instigators of planned change must look ahead to see if, in practical terms, those who facilitate change and those who will be affected by the new behaviour can adapt to the proposed change. This issue can be helped by adopting a systems perspective, whether it be one arising out of the 'hard approach' of systems engineering or operational research or the softer approaches of social psychology and organisational development. All systems approaches to change try to analyse and understand the processes and the implications of change, on subsystems and others, that occur within the problem being addressed by the planned change. (Mabey and Mayon-White, 1993)

Critique of force field analysis

Lewin's model is said to provide a simple general framework for understanding organisational change. However, planned change is not a simplistic process nor is it a linear and static concept. Lewin's model assumes the planned change occurs between discrete fixed states, 'as a matter of being in State 1 at Time 1 and State 2 at Time 2' (Kanter, Stein and Jick, 1992). Kanter *et al.* go on to say that the only reason that this 'wildly inappropriate' model has prospered is because of its ability to offer managers a straight forward approach to planned organisational change, by simplifying this extremely complex issue into 'a child's formula'. In reality organisations are never frozen. They are in a constant state of flux like a river. They are influenced internally and externally by many different personalities and institutions. As a result each of the separate steps defined by Lewin does not in reality occur in isolation. They are interdependent upon one another in a continuous iterative process. Organisational change is a multidimensional interrelated process. Planned change is a means of channelling the organisation's direction in the correct way forward perceived by key members. The approach, be it pluralist or unitarist, will determine who the key members are in the organisation. If the organisation takes a pluralist perspective it will appreciate that people within the organisation, be they members, managers or staff, all have different needs, goals, ideas. To function well the organisation needs to recognise, appreciate and build developments that take account of these realities. In contrast organisations tend when seeking to implement change to adopt, often unwittingly, a unitarist approach whereby effectiveness is underpinned by the key senior management's perceptions of 'one best way of doing things' which limits individuals' capacities to contribute. Then senior management wonder why attempts at change end in failure. How often have we heard a Chief Officer confidently explain a change such as management delegation being brought about in her/his department, but when you investigate the reality at junior manager or even middle manager level there is a somewhat different picture. A range of responses from 'yes, it is operating here', to 'I know about it but implementation is blocked in this section' to 'I have not seen this in operation' or 'I don't know anything about that' may emerge. With increased fragmentation this range of responses is quite likely to occur unless a lot of work goes into reducing such outcomes.

It is, however, useful to remember that Lewin's model emphasises the relationship between the external environment and the internal organ-isational environment. In a practical sense it offers practitioners a useful framework for considering and analysing the external and internal driving and restraining forces that are affecting their organisations progress at any given time.

One ought nevertheless to register a cautionary note in favour of the restraining forces that counteract an organisation's desire to change. Change affects individuals and we know that people have a need for stability in their lives. Thus in certain circumstances restraining forces may be beneficial when seeking to redress the balance of a philosophy which encourages continuous radical change.

Lewin's model of planned change, like the majority of the organisational change literature, typically describes change as a three-part process that takes the flawed organisation through an arduous transition stage to the closing stage of refreezing or stabilisation. See Figure 8.1 below for examples.

Whilst models are useful, in reality change is a far more complex issue, underlined by the high failure rate not only in implementing change but in ensuring the change is sustained. The models analysed and outlined above are what Kanter, Stein and Jick (1992) call a 'prescription' for creating temporary stability. The models, like many other planned change models tend to put forward models geared towards 'experts', consultants being the main catalyst or playing a major role in the change process. The models

MODEL	PROCESS		
Lewin (1947)	Unfreezing	Changing	Refreezing
Beckhard and Harris (1987)	Present State	Transition State	Future State
Beer *et al.* (1980)	Dissatisfaction X	Process X	Model
Kanter (1983)	Departures from tradition and crises	Strategic decisions and prime movers	Action vehicles and institutional-isation
Tichy and Devanna (1986)	Act I Awakening	Act II Mobilising	Act III (Epilogue) Reinforcing
Nadler and Tushman (1989)	Energising	Envisioning	Enabling

Figure 8.1: Models of Planned Change

provide a framework but give limited information on the types of methods to be employed in order to achieve planned change. They take little account of the fact that organisations vary drastically in structure, size, products, services, communications and people. What worked for one organisation will not necessarily work for the next.

Context of change

One of the most important weaknesses or flaws in the above models is the failure to recognise the context in which such changes take place. These changes do not occur in a motionless environment but in one that is constantly moving. The models tend to provide a framework of discrete steps or stages. At any one time an organisation is being pulled in various directions. Internal or external forces do not exert their pressure in a unitary manner on task units, divisions, projects, interest groups which are themselves in motion. Organisations are comprised of multiple 'clusters of activity sets' (Kanter, Stein and Jick, 1992), multiple stakeholders, whose own membership, ownership and goals are constantly changing and as a result are constantly influencing organisational life through various routes. In local government CCT reinforces this point with the changing focus from blue collar workers to white collar services teams. This new focus means that several more departments have to consider the implications for service delivery: there will be differing considerations for example in a Planning and Transport Department as against a Legal Department but both will impact separately and jointly on County Councils where both functions lie.

Organisations are a 'coalition of interests and a network of activities' (Kanter, Stein and Jick, 1992). Changes are not always guided by the organisational leaders or principal stakeholders. Political interests also come into play in the identification and labelling of change. As Kanter (1983) says, we should always ask who has a stake in declaring something to be 'new and different'. Managers seeking to implement planned change need to be aware of the nature of the various activity sets and work through them to ensure adoption of planned change'. Local authorities are moving away from the hierarchical bureaucratic structures to teams, business units and project groups working together in a flatter structure. Therefore to suggest a downward set of commands to implement planned change, as is the case with the majority of the models, is unrealistic.

Stability in an organisation, defined as the quasi-stationary equilibrium by Lewin, is also an ideal rather than a reality. Stability for a local government in today's globalising economic environment has to be a smooth changing flow. Forces internal and external such as shifts in government regulations or internal competition, can render one planned change obsolete whilst at the same time accelerating the speed of another. Therefore to be realistic and effective models of planned organisation change have to be in a constant flow. Change can no longer be classified as moving from one state to another state; in many terms models need to be in a constant state of change if they wish to mirror realistically today's organisations. This point has been well made by Peters and Waterman in *Thriving on Chaos* (1992)

■ PROPOSED CHANGE, CURRENTLY WHAT DO WE KNOW?

Recent literature on planned change in various situations (Dunphy and Stace, 1989; Nadler and Tushman, 1989; Allaire and Firsirotu, 1985; Goodman *et al.*, 1982), consultancy and practitioner experiences in local governments have emphasised important factors that change managers need to take into account.

- While it is true that change must be planned, it is better to conceive of it as a dynamic integrative collaborative process which seeks to engage people in clusters of activity moving in a common strategic direction.

- Change agents must recognise the realities of organisational power, control and resistance. Change will not happen unless the political dynamics of change are addressed.

- Change agents must identify enough powerful groups who will gain from the proposed changes in a variety of ways and thus offer their support to the changes.

- Change agents must always be questioned in relation to the strength of why do it, against the strength of why not.

- Change agents that have focused on the external (threat/opportunity) as in local government legislation, local Government Review and then given leadership and direction in response to the threat/opportunity are more likely to be successful. This applies to public and private sector.

- Change agents must get people involved, but in the right actions.

- Change agents must not cause the organisation as a system to be out of balance, people must be supported in understanding and operating in their changing working environment.

- Change agents should communicate continuously.

- Change agents need to encourage learning and reviewing.

- Change agents are constantly asking—what has really changed around here?

- Change agents must create an awareness of the need to change.

The above list recognises what we know to be true in local government, that change is an ongoing dynamic process that affects the culture, norms and values of the organisation and, to be successful, has to be a learning process for both the top and bottom of organisational structures. The change process is very much dependent on the successful understanding and appreciation of the importance of culture, norms, and values (conscious and subconscious) at the individual, group and organisation level as determinants of successful change. There is one interesting example of this told to me by a Director of Social Services in the mid-1980s. His department had introduced delegated budgets to residential homes. About two months into the process he was visiting several homes to see how the scheme was operating on the ground. One residential home manager was very proud because he had not spent any money.

Practical experience of the change processes has taught us the importance of these factors but what do you do if you are wishing to introduce a particular change initiative yourself? I would return to two key words and they are **content** and **process**. Any manager of change has to be conscious at all times that change operates dynamically and simultaneously at these two levels. The content is the *what* of the plan. The process is the *how* of the plan. Another important element to remember is that change takes root within different locations in the organisation and therefore the pace of implementation will differ. Change is implemented by people; how does the manager get them involved?

■ MANAGING AN EFFECTIVE CHANGE PROCESS

Thinking about the different change initiatives I have been involved in and observing and learning about other change processes the practical advice in my view can be stated as the need to adopt a participatory approach, which from the beginning involves those effected by change and takes account of views from the bottom up. Change processes need to address five major sets of activities within a participatory strategy. These are:

- **Creating a favourable climate for change**
  developing an awareness of the need to change
  overcoming the resistance to change

- **Creating a shared understanding of the way forward**
  clear direction, vision
  valued outcomes
  valued framework
  mid-term goals

- **Developing political support**
  assessing your own power
  identifying where the power lies, key stakeholders
  influencing stakeholders

- **Managing the transition**
  planning activities with key players which demonstrate commitment to the chosen direction

- **Supporting and maintaining the change**
  supporting the change in terms of resources
  developing new competencies and skills
  reinforcing new behaviours

Creating a favourable climate for change

The main emphasis here is that organisations/departments/divisions/sections etc. can be very good at ignoring change in the environment in which they operate. They do not always see the need to change. The change manager's skill is to break through that threshold of awareness and show the difference between the current position and the desired future state. The desired future state has to be communicated clearly and comprehensively. People who will be affected by the changes should be actively involved in planning and implementing the changes and support must be offered to those who feel threatened by the change. Staff always have expectations about change. If you can communicate realistic positive expectations about organisational changes it helps with commitment.

Creating a shared understanding of the way forward

This is where the change manager has to play a clear leadership role in helping the participants in the change process to articulate the mission of their organisation or sub-unit in changing. To be of real value this must articulate main purpose or reason for existing; basic beliefs; values; priorities; strengths and the image you wish to portray. Of equal importance is the need to state, in terms of valued outcomes, what the vision means. In terms of human resources this could be valuing staff through development and training or valuing service to the public in terms of quality. The valued outcomes serve as goals and standards for assessing performance (*see* Chapter 6). It is also necessary to articulate the way forward in terms of what the structural framework of the change may look like. This could be as broad as decentralisation or structuring reward according to performance or as specific as citizen's charters. I have also found it useful to state mid-term goals which are more specific than the overall direction of the change. So for example if the change was about restructuring a department and developing new ways of working, a mid-term goal would be, following communication and consultation with concerned staff, to have replaced old individual job descriptions with new job spaces by an agreed date. These job spaces would state a person's key result areas and expected measurable outcomes. This offers people the security to move forward .

Developing political support

Local government has of course large 'P' in the sense of party politics and small 'p' organisational politics. Nevertheless, taking an overall political perspective, an authority can be seen as loosely structured coalitions of individuals, and groups with different views and agenda. In this context the change manager must decide where their own power lies. This may come from expert knowledge, or control of particular systems, or power of personality. Once you have decided what these are then you need to identify the significant stakeholders who have an interest in your change initiative. It is often useful to make a list of the winners and losers in your change initiative and whom they can influence positively or negatively. You need more winners than losers for a successful change. As change manager you must then work hard at gaining support so that you have that vital critical mass to carry you forward.

I have seen this managed exquisitely in one particular Council where the control changed from Conservative to Labour, but Labour were depending on two independents for control. The new Labour Leader began his term of office by stating publicly that he valued the contributions made by the former administration, and at the same time he made it clear that Labour would broaden the values that had underpinned previous policy decisions to incorporate their own priorities for local democracy. This statement was widely circulated to elected members and senior officers. There then followed a series of meetings and consultations on how to agree the Council's new key priorities. It was agreed that, to begin with, all leading Chairmen, Chairwomen and Chief Officers should meet together with a facilitator to develop the Council's key priorities. The outcome of these sessions was then taken by the Leader for wider consultation with his own party from which emerged a final draft which was then shared with the leaders of the two opposition parties. When the key priorities were presented to the Council's Policy and Resources Committee they were accepted unanimously. Just as importantly Chief Officers immediately began the process of ensuring the translation and implementation of these priorities into their departmental objectives.

Managing the transition

This is really the implementation process and is closely connected to the need to gain political support for your change initiative as well as the need to demonstrate through actual activities that the change process is being implemented. Here you need to draw a road map or path which shows enough people the journey they are embarking on and the destination. It is really important to appreciate that we may have a common destination but there are several routes. Another key factor to be aware of is that different groups even within one department, are at different stages of development in their activities. This is even more true for one authority. The chances of change initiatives being effectively implemented are increased if the interventions begins with where people are. The following example from a County Council wishing to improve the current performance of individuals by clarifying accountabilities and responsibilities will illustrate this point.

The Chief Executive and his Chief Officers' Management Team recognised that the authorities approach to performance management needed clarification to increase the effectiveness of service delivery. The whole area of performance management was explored from the way members review performance to different ways in which individual performance can be improved. This resulted in the introduction of new political processes for the review of Chief Officer and departmental performance in a more frequent and focused manner. At departmental level Chief Officers chose different routes in consultation and participation with their departments as to how best to improve performance in their departments. The options chosen by departments included going for Investors in People Awards, Individual Performance Appraisal Schemes, Performance Management focusing on Key Result Areas; and Staff Development Schemes.

This example demonstrates the importance of ensuring commitment and putting in place a structure where the change initiative will obviously have the support and the power to guide the change process.

Supporting and maintaining the change

Change initiatives need additional resources and enormous amounts of energy devoted to encouraging people to sustain the change. This requires the commitment and leadership of the change manager. It is often a good idea for the change manager to have the help and support of an outsider in observing and monitoring the change process or in introducing the process in collaboration with the change manager. Change usually requires people to behave in a different way. They must be supported in this by rewarding the new behaviours either in terms of monetary or non-monetary rewards. The implications of people requiring new skills and knowledge for the new environment must be addressed in the process. This last point links nicely to how individuals feel about change processes.

■ THE INDIVIDUAL AND CHANGE

In many ways individuals' behaviour is dependent upon the expectations and aspirations they associate with the outcome of their relationship with the organisation. Each individual usually has a set of unstated results that she/he expects to achieve from the relationship with the organisation and vice versa. These unstated expectations of individuals are known as **psychological contracts**. The individual is motivated to maintain the relationship whilst her/his expectations are met. However, planned change arouses uncertainty in the individual, and although they may clearly understand the implications of change for their legal contract with the organisation, they are often uncertain how change will affect the expectations of their unstated psychological contract.

Psychological contracts

The concept of the psychological contract is a useful one in understanding the dynamics of and resistance to change. Within the work environment individuals have employment contracts, but a kind of implicit contract emerges over time which is psychological in nature and is related to the implicit expectations individuals have of the organisation and the variety of expectations the organisation may have of the individual employee. For example people may come to work to feel secure, make contact with interesting people, achieve status and recognition in the world of work. Such expectations are not part of the formal employee contract. On the other hand the organisation often has expectations of its employees which are not always explicitly stated. The official contract may say a 44-hour week, but the expectation may be that, to progress, the individual has to work much longer hours to achieve promotion. The interesting feature of psychological contracts in the workplace is that they commence at the very beginning when the employee first enters the organisation. The contract develops over time as the person begins to understand the nature and perceived requirements of the organisation. We can think of this in terms of economic and social exchange. The whole person comes to work with a variety of needs and expectations. Organisations which recognise this fact try hard to achieve organisation outcomes such as quality of service while seeking to facilitate the achievement of the individual goals of its members. Individual goals can be as diverse as maximum pay, status, internal satisfaction, or friendship. This whole area is often very simply called motivation but it is a vital area for effective performance. Such psychological contracts can be threatened by the introduction of a change process that upsets the individuals' interpretation of the world of work. Disparity between individual and organisational expectations can lead to resistance on the part of individuals to the change process.

Often, with a change process, individuals feel they are being asked to move away from a comfort zone of clear known authority and expertise, coupled with core competencies and skills which together gave them confidence in their ability to perform their organisational role. Change often asks people to move to undefined areas of responsibility with new demands and requirements that need new skills and competencies. The wider and longer the time frame allowed for this uncertainty the more likely the change manager is to experience individual resistance.

Some individual elements of resistance to planned change

One of the most damaging forms of resistance to planned change is lack of participation in and commitment to proposed changes which can occur even when people have had the opportunities to participate. Resistance to planned change stems from a variety of sources. Some of the sources are individual, while others involve the nature and structure of the organisation. It is important for change managers to be aware of the main causes for individuals resistance to change. Individual factors include:

- loss of control
- fear of the unknown
- lack of job security
- economic loss in the form of eliminated jobs, reduced pay
- knowledge and skill obsolescence

Individuals tend to develop norms and values for individual behaviour within the group environment which have their effect on task performance. The more cohesive and attractive the group setting the more pressure/ influence that group can exert on members to resist change when these norms and values are challenged.

Individuals work for economic and social reasons therefore individuals may still resist change even if there are no economic losses. In simple terms if reorganisation means 'I no longer have my window seat', or 'I no longer sit next to my friend' or 'it is more difficult to park my car', the individual may take some convincing to see the benefits.

Individuals are concerned about their own competence in the new job. They perceive the change as a threat to their current power or influence.

Resistance is not just a case of cause and effect. It usually is far more-deep rooted than the surface appearance, it is a complex mix of emotional, factual and historical issues. Resistance can be essentially split into two types (Schein, 1985):

- **Systemic resistance** arises from lack of appropriate information, knowledge, skill and lack of managerial capacity.
- **Behavioural resistance** describes the resistance deriving from assumptions, perceptions, and reactions of individual or groups.

One is cognitive, based on knowledge and rational decision-making, the other emotional. An emotion-based resistance such as low trust is much more difficult to overcome than a lack of information or misinterpretation. Thus some types of resistance are easier to overcome than others.

■ IMPLICATIONS FOR YOU AS MANAGER

I have stressed the need for an integrative and a participatory approach to planned change to be adopted by local authorities. Essentially managers must be capable of gaining Member and officer commitment to new ideas if they are going to survive in complex and competing environments. This means being able to communicate with and understand the different perspectives that exist within any hierarchical organisation. People need to be supported through any change process so that they can learn to master the challenges of the new situation, as opposed to fearing it. Thus, while it is perfectly legitimate for senior management to set purpose and direction, this needs to be tempered with a planned participative approach to implementation. Dialogue, communication, consultation and appropriate support for staff are essential ingredients in any successful sustainable change initiative.

References

Allaire, Y. and Firsirotu, M. (1985) 'How to Implement Radical Strategies in Large Organisations', *Sloan Management Review* (Winter, pp.19–34)

Beckhard, R. and Harris, R. T. (1987) *Organisational Transitions: Managing Complex Change*, Addison-Wesley, Reading Mass.

Beer, M., Eisenstat, R.A. and Spector, B. (1990) 'Why Change Programs Don't Change', *Harvard Business Review* (68, pp.158–66)

Dunphy, D.C. and Stace, D. (1989) *Evolution or Transformation? Incremental versus Transformational Ideologies for Organisational Change.* Australian Graduate School of Management, University of New South Wales

Goodman, P.S. *et al.* (1982) *Change in Organisations.* Jossey-Bass, San Francisco

Kanter, R.M., Stein, B. and Jick, T. (1992) *The Challenge of Organisational Change*. Free Press, New York

Kanter, R.M. (1983) *The Change Masters: Innovation and Entrepreneurship in the American Corporation*. Simon & Schuster, New York

Kanter, R.M. (1985) 'Managing the Human Side of Change', *Management Review* (April)

Lewin, K. (1947) 'Frontiers in Group Dynamics', *Human Relations* (1, pp.5–41

Mabey, C. and Mayon-White, B. (1993) *Managing Change*. Paul Chapman Publishing, London

Nadler, D. and Tushman, M. (1989) 'Organisational Framebending: Principles for Managing Reorientation', *Academy of Management Executive* (1, 145–53)

Peters, T.J. and Waterman, R.H. (1989) *Thriving on Chaos: Handbook for a management revolution*. Pan in association with Macmillan, London

Schein, E. H. (1985) *Organisational Culture and Leadership*. Jossey-Bass, San Francisco

Tichy, N. and Devanna, M. (1986) *The Transformational Leader*. John Wiley & Sons, New York

KING ALFRED'S COLLEGE
LIBRARY